# Buonissimo!

RYLAND
PETERS
& SMALL
LONDON NEW YORK

# Buonissimo!

easy modern recipes for traditional Italian cooking

Silvana Franco   Ursula Ferrigno   Clare Ferguson   Elsa Petersen-Schepelern

First published in the United States in 2002
by Ryland Peters & Small, Inc.
519 Broadway, 5th Floor
New York, NY 10012
www.rylandpeters.com

Text © Clare Ferguson, Ursula Ferrigno, Ryland
Peters & Small and Elsa Petersen-Schepelern 2002
Design and photographs
© Ryland Peters & Small 2002
10 9 8 7 6 5 4 3 2 1

Library of Congress Cataloging-in-Publication Data

Buonissimo! : delicious modern recipes
                for traditional Italian cooking.
      p. cm
   Includes index.
   ISBN 1-84172-335-5
   1. Cookery, Italian.
TX723 .B784 2002
641.5945--dc21                    2002066757

Printed and bound in China

**Senior Designer** Susan Downing
**Commissioning Editor** Elsa Petersen-Schepelern
**Editors** Kathy Steer, Jennifer Herman
**Production** Tamsin Curwood
**Art Director** Gabriella Le Grazie
**Publishing Director** Alison Starling
**Indexer** Hilary Bird

**Notes**
All spoon measurements are level.

All eggs are large, unless otherwise specified.
Uncooked or partly cooked eggs should not be served
to the very young, the very old, those with
compromised immune systems, or to pregnant women.

To sterilize preserving jars, wash the jars in hot, soapy
water and rinse in boiling water. Put into a large
saucepan and add water to cover. With the lid on, bring
the water to a boil and continue boiling for 15 minutes.
Turn off the heat, then leave the jars in the hot water
until just before they are to be filled. Invert the jars
onto clean kitchen towels to dry. Sterilize the lids for
5 minutes by boiling. Jars should be filled and sealed
while still hot.

Recipes in this book have previously been published in
other Ryland Peters & Small books (see page 144).

# contents

# buonissimo ...

Italian is everyone's favorite food—even if you can't boil an egg, it's a good bet that you can cook pasta, stir in a sauce, toss a salad, and pour a glass of wine. So that's Italian—you know you love it, and you can make it.

*Buonissimo* builds on those skills you didn't know you had—with easy, modern versions of Italy's great traditional recipes. Cook your own pizza—from scratch. Make delicious antipasti to serve before the meal. Prepare fish, meat, and poultry in the simple, easy flavorful way Italians do. Serve them with Italian vegetables—then follow up with those splendid desserts for which Italy is so famous. Cook Italian for family meals, casual lunches, or elegant dinner parties: *Buonissimo!* will show you how.

*Buonissimo* means the "absolute best" in Italian, and the recipes you'll find in this book are some of the best Italian dishes, certainly they are some of our favorites. However, they're just a selection. Try them, and see how easy it is—we hope they'll give you confidence and encourage you to try more Italian cooking.

antipasti

These simple savory cookies are delicious with anchovy, but you can try other variations, such as sun-dried tomato pesto or a pinch of hot red pepper flakes.

# anchovy
# pinwheels

2 oz. canned anchovy fillets, finely chopped

1 lb. puff pastry dough, ready-to-roll or frozen and thawed

all-purpose flour, for dusting

1 egg, beaten

2 nonstick baking trays, brushed with water

**Makes about 60**

Using a mortar and pestle or small bowl and the back of a spoon, mash the anchovies with 1 teaspoon water to form a paste. Keep adding water until a smooth, brushable liquid results.

Put the dough onto a lightly floured work surface and roll out to a rectangle about $1/8$ inch thick.

Using a pastry brush, brush the anchovy mixture all over the surface (not too thick, or the taste will be too strong), then brush the far edge with beaten egg. Starting at the edge nearest you, roll up the dough into a sausage shape about 1 inch thick and press the egg-washed edge to seal. Chill in the refrigerator for 30 minutes.

Using a sharp knife, cut the sausage crosswise into $1/8$-inch slices and arrange apart on the baking trays.

Bake, in batches if necessary, in a preheated oven at 400°F for about 10–12 minutes until crisp and golden. Remove from the oven, let cool for about 3 minutes, then transfer to a wire rack to cool completely. Serve immediately or store in an airtight container for up to 3 days.

Homemade cheese straws taste much better than the store-bought variety, and are very easy to make.

## spice-speckled
# cheese straws

1 cup all-purpose flour, plus extra for dusting

½ teaspoon salt

1 teaspoon dry mustard powder

2 oz. Cheddar cheese, grated

2 tablespoons freshly grated Parmesan cheese

6 tablespoons unsalted butter, chilled and cut into small pieces

1 egg yolk

juice of ½ lemon

paprika, for dusting (optional)

*2 baking trays, greased*

**Makes 36**

Put the flour, salt, mustard, and cheeses into a food processor and pulse to mix. Add the butter and pulse until the mixture resembles fine bread crumbs.

Mix the egg yolk and lemon juice in a small bowl, then pour into the processor with the motor running. Stop mixing when the mixture forms a dough. Transfer to a lightly floured surface and knead briefly to form a ball.

Roll out the dough to a rectangle ⅛ inch thick. Using a hot, sharp knife, cut into strips ½ inch wide and about 3 inches long. Twist into spirals and arrange well apart on the baking trays.

Bake in a preheated oven at 350°F for 10 minutes until golden. Remove from the oven, dust with paprika, if using, then let cool on the baking trays. Serve immediately or store in an airtight container for up to 3 days.

Crostini and bruschetta are the easiest of all antipasti—just good bread, toasted, then topped with whatever you please. Make big ones (bruschette) for lunch, or lots of little ones (crostini) as bite-size party snacks.

# crostini and bruschetta

**Crostini**

1 baguette

your choice of toppings from the list below

**Bruschetta**

Italian bread of your choice, such as ciabatta, focaccia, puglièse, or crusty country bread

1–2 garlic cloves, halved

*a large baking tray*

**Makes about 30**

To make crostini, cut a baguette into ½-inch slices and arrange on a baking tray. Bake in a preheated oven at 400°F until lightly golden, about 3–4 minutes. Don't let them become too crisp or they will break when people take a bite.

Remove from the oven and let cool on a wire rack. They can be kept in an airtight container for up to 1 week. When ready to serve, crisp them again in a preheated oven at 400°F for a few minutes. Remove from the heat, then add your choice of toppings—if using cheese you want to melt, put it on top before returning to the oven.

To make bruschetta, cut thick slices of bread, then rub with a cut garlic clove. Put the slices into a stove-top grill pan or under a preheated broiler and cook until golden brown. Alternatively, cook over a medium-hot outdoor grill until golden brown.

**Toppings** Choose no more than 2–3 toppings or the flavors will be too confused and, if making bite-size crostini, the toppings will fall off. Choose from the pizza toppings on page 15, or other choices include:

• Finely sliced prosciutto

• Parmesan shavings

• Caperberries or capers

• Cherry tomatoes, halved

• Oven-dried tomatoes with Fontina cheese

• Flaked char-grilled tuna with scallions

• Fontina cheese, pancetta or prosciutto strips, and cracked black pepper

• Smoked or poached salmon

• Char-grilled peppers or eggplant

• Anchovies with melted mozzarella.

Mini versions of Italian pizza are perfect for parties. Use part-baked pizza bases from an Italian gourmet store, and cut out mini rounds using a cookie cutter. The same store can provide a selection of delicious ready-made toppings, and you can also make others.

# mini pizzas

4 Italian pizza bases,
about 10 inches diameter
(or see variation)

olive oil, for brushing

your choice of toppings
from the list
below

*1½ inch cookie cutter*

*several nonstick
baking trays*

**Makes 28**

Using the cookie cutter, cut out rounds from the pizza bases, then arrange on several baking trays spaced well apart. Brush with olive oil and add your choice of toppings. Bake in a preheated oven at 400°F for about 5 minutes or until piping hot.

If using cheese toppings, brush the pizza bases with olive oil and bake in a preheated oven at 400°F for about 3 minutes first, then add cheese toppings of your choice and heat through for 1–2 minutes until softly melted, but not running away.

**Variation**

Instead of store-bought pizza bases, you can use slices of bread, toasted, then cut out with the cookie cutter.

**Toppings** Don't use more than 3–4 ingredients on each pizza or the flavors will be too complicated. Choose from the crostini toppings on page 12, or other choices include:

• Red pesto brushed over the surface, then topped with a curl of char-grilled yellow pepper and half an oven-dried garlic-spiked tomato, sprinkled with fresh thyme leaves

• Fontina cheese with anchovy and a dot of red pesto

• Char-grilled yellow bell pepper with roasted baby artichokes

• Mozzarella, anchovy, and dried oregano

• Sautéed mushrooms with Gruyère, Gorgonzola, and mozzarella cheeses.

*Bagna cauda* means "hot bath," and this dip from Piedmont in northwest Italy is mellow, smooth, and intensely flavorful. The crisp, sweet, mild vegetables offset the salty flavor of the sauce.

# bagna cauda

1 stick unsalted butter

6–8 garlic cloves, crushed to a purée

½ cup extra virgin olive oil

4 oz. canned anchovy fillets, drained, chopped, and mashed

**Your choice of:**

red, yellow, or orange bell peppers (but not green), cut into 8 wedges and seeded

white wax peppers, halved and seeded

celery stalks

chicory (Belgian endive)

trevise (radicchio)

inner leaves from romaine lettuce

scallions

baby asparagus

cauliflower florets

broccoli florets, quartered lengthwise

fennel bulbs, cut into wedges lengthwise

sprigs of flat-leaf parsley

**Serves 4–8**

Put the butter and garlic into a nonstick skillet and heat gently until the butter has melted. Transfer to a blender and add the olive oil and anchovies. Purée for 2–3 minutes, then transfer to a serving bowl. The bowl of dip should be kept hot over a low candle flame.

Surround the hot dip with the vegetables and serve.

**Note** The traditional method is to put the butter and puréed garlic into a shallow terracotta dish and stir for 5–10 minutes over low to medium heat. Add the anchovy fillets and mash over the heat. Add the oil, reheat gently, then serve as in main recipe.

Vegetables are delicious grilled—the charred bits have a delightfully smoky flavor. Use typical Mediterranean vegetables, bursting with ripeness and color.

# grilled vegetables

4 medium yellow squash

4 medium green zucchini

4 long thin eggplants or 8 small Japanese eggplants

2 long red peppers (Cubanelle), halved and seeded, stems intact if possible

2 long yellow or orange peppers (Cubanelle), halved and seeded, stems intact if possible

2 large, mild red chiles, halved and seeded (optional)

olive oil, for coating

sea salt and freshly ground black pepper

**Marinade**

2 cups extra virgin olive oil

sea salt and whole black peppercorns, crushed

4 sprigs of fresh thyme or oregano, coarsely chopped

½ cup white wine vinegar

*a stove-top grill pan*

**Serves 8**

To prepare the vegetables, cut the squash and zucchini lengthwise into ⅛-inch slices and cut the eggplant lengthwise into ½-inch slices. Put the pepper halves, chiles, if using, squash, zucchini, and eggplant into a large plastic bag. Add some olive oil, salt, and pepper and shake to coat the vegetables with oil.

Heat a stove-top grill pan over medium heat until hot. Add the peppers skin side down, put a heavy weight such as a saucepan on top, and cook until dark and charred with marks. Turn the peppers over, put the saucepan back on top, and cook until tender. If you want to remove the skins, put the peppers into a small saucepan and cover with a lid—the skins will steam off and you won't lose any of the delicious juices. Put the chiles, if using, onto the preheated stove-top grill pan and cook for about 2 minutes on each side until dark and charred with marks. Using a sharp knife, slice the chiles lengthwise into fine strips.

Working in batches, put the squash, zucchini, and eggplants onto the grill pan and cook until tender and charred with marks—the squash and zucchini will take about 2 minutes on each side, the eggplant about 2–3 minutes on each side, or until cooked all the way through (very important for eggplant). Put all the vegetables into separate containers.

To make the marinade, put the olive oil, salt, pepper, and thyme or oregano into a small saucepan and heat, stirring constantly. Remove from the heat and carefully add the vinegar (take care or the oil may spatter). Pour over the vegetables. Let marinate for at least 30 minutes, then serve.

Alternatively, the vegetables may be packed into sterilized preserving jars (see page 4), covered with the olive oil mixture, and refrigerated. When ready to serve, let return to room temperature first.

Bell peppers are ideal ingredients in antipasti: they respond well to broiling and roasting, two methods that develop the natural sugars. Mixed with salty anchovies and sharp pickled caperberries or capers, they really come into their own. This recipe is from southern Italy—easy, elegant, and delicious.

# peperoni farciti

4 red or yellow bell peppers, quartered lengthwise and seeded

16 canned anchovy fillets, rinsed and drained

16 caperberries or 2 tablespoons capers, rinsed and drained

a small bunch of fresh marjoram or oregano, chopped

2 tablespoons extra virgin olive oil

freshly ground black pepper

**Serves 4**

Arrange the bell pepper wedges in a large roasting dish or pan.

Using kitchen shears or a small knife, cut each anchovy fillet lengthwise into 2 strips. Put 2 strips into each pepper wedge. Add a caperberry or a share of the capers to each wedge and sprinkle with the chopped herbs and olive oil.

Roast, uncovered, towards the top of a preheated oven at 350°F for about 20–30 minutes or until the peppers are wrinkled, aromatic, and beginning to char at the edges. Serve hot, warm, or cool, sprinkled with black pepper.

**Note** Don't use green bell peppers for this dish—they lack the sweetness of red or yellow ones.

Both these olive recipes will keep very well in a cool, dark place for weeks—or even months, if they get the chance. *Sott'olio* means "under oil." They are excellent served with the crostini on page 12.

# black olives
## sott'olio

¼ cup coriander seeds, crushed

2 tablespoons black peppercorns

8 garlic cloves, halved lengthwise

1 lb. black olives in brine, drained, patted dry, and pricked with a fork or sharp knife

zest of 1 large unwaxed lemon, removed in long strips

3 cups extra virgin olive oil

1½-quart preserving jar or 3 x 2-cup bottles, sterilized (page 4)

**Makes 1 large or 3 small bottles**

Put the coriander seeds, peppercorns, and garlic into a dry skillet and cook over gentle heat, shaking and toasting until aromatic: do not let scorch. Stir in the olives and cook for 2–3 minutes.

Put the still-hot sterilized bottles onto a folded cloth or wooden board. Using a sterilized spoon, transfer the mixture into the bottle(s). Push in the lemon zest with sterilized metal tongs.

Put the oil into a saucepan and heat to 350°F or until a small cube of bread turns golden brown in 40 seconds. Let cool for 2 minutes, then pour the oil carefully into the bottle(s) to cover the olives. Let cool, uncovered. Top up with any unused oil, cover, and seal tightly. Store in a cool, dark cupboard until ready to serve.

If you have fennel flowers in your garden, use the whole seed heads for this dish. Otherwise, use fennel seeds, which are available from most supermarkets.

# green olives
## with fennel

1 lb. preserved green olives, washed and dried with paper towels, then pricked with a fork

2 cups extra virgin olive oil

2 whole heads of fresh garlic, halved crosswise

4–8 fresh fennel flower heads, seeds intact (optional)

3 tablespoons black peppercorns, cracked or coarsely crushed

2 tablespoons fennel seeds

1 teaspoon cloves

1-quart preserving jar, sterilized (page 4)

**Makes 1 quart**

Pack half the olives loosely into the sterilized bottle(s) using sterilized metal tongs or a spoon. Put the olive oil into a saucepan and heat to 350°F or until a small cube of bread turns golden in 40 seconds.

Using a slotted spoon, lower the halved garlic heads and fennel flower heads into the oil. Let them sizzle for about 30 seconds, then lift out and divide between the bottle(s). Sprinkle in the peppercorns, fennel seeds, and cloves. Top up with the remaining olives. Pour the hot oil carefully over the olives until covered. Let cool for 2 minutes, then pour the remaining oil carefully into the bottle(s) until filled. Let cool, uncovered and undisturbed. Seal tightly and store in a cool, dark cupboard until ready to serve.

This recipe can be served on garlic toasts, or with pasta, rice, or even polenta. It is delectably easy and good, whichever way you choose. When you buy mussels, keep them cool and use them the same day. Scrub the mussels thoroughly with a small brush and use only those that are tightly closed.

# mussels
## with garlic, parsley, and lemon

2 lb. large mussels, scrubbed

4 garlic cloves,
crushed and chopped

2 tablespoons extra virgin olive oil

¼ cup white wine

a long strip of zest and freshly
squeezed juice of
1 lemon

a small bunch of fresh fennel
fronds or parsley, chopped

freshly ground black pepper

crusty bread, to serve

**Serves 4**

Pull off and discard the beards from the mussels. Tap any open mussels against the work surface: if they don't close immediately, discard them. Scrub the mussels briefly and rinse again under cold running water.

Put the mussels into a heavy saucepan, add the garlic, olive oil, white wine, lemon zest, and juice, and bring to a boil. Cover with a lid, reduce the heat to medium, and cook, undisturbed, for 3–4 minutes or until the shells are open and the mussels plumply cooked (discard any mussels that don't open).

Stir in half the chopped fennel or parsley, then cover again. Turn off the heat and leave for 1 minute. Remove and discard the empty half-shells from the mussels.

Transfer the mussels into 1 large or 4 small bowls or plates. Sprinkle the remaining chopped fennel or parsley on top and add generous grinds of black pepper. Eat hot or warm, with crusty bread to mop up the delicious juices.

**Variation**

Add 1 large tomato, cut into tiny cubes, and omit the lemon zest.

Clams are very popular in Italy and are used in many different ways, all simple and delicious. For instance, *pasta con le vongole*—pasta with clam sauce (page 78)—is an all-time favorite.

# clams
## with chile parsley sauce

2 lb., small clams, scrubbed, rinsed, and drained

¼ cup extra virgin olive oil

1 teaspoon hot red pepper flakes or crushed dried chiles

4 garlic cloves, chopped

1 onion, finely chopped

½ cup dry or sweet white vermouth

freshly ground black pepper

a handful of fresh parsley, chopped, plus 4–6 leaves, to serve (optional)

**Serves 4–6**

Put the clams, olive oil, red pepper flakes, garlic, onion, vermouth, and black pepper into a large saucepan. Bring to a boil, cover tightly with a lid, reduce the heat, and let steam for 4–6 minutes.

Stir in the chopped parsley, then cover again. Turn off the heat, let steam for a further 1 minute, then serve, topped with a fresh parsley leaf, if using.

**Note** Canned or bottled clams (*vongole*) are widely available in Italian gourmet stores: useful if you can't find any fresh clams. If using them, drain the liquid into the pan, add all the remaining ingredients except the clams, bring to a boil, and reduce to about 1 cup. Add the drained clams, then steam just until the clams have been heated through. Serve as in the main recipe.

White cannellini beans are traditional in Tuscany, but you can use any dried beans. I like chickpeas, and the pretty color of green flageolets (canned, unripe cannellinis, available in some Italian stores) looks wonderful. Fresh tuna can be expensive, so this recipe is a good way of making one steak stretch a little further.

# tonno e fagioli

1 large tuna steak, about 8 oz., or 2 cans good-quality tuna, about 6 oz. each, drained

⅓ cup olive oil, plus extra for brushing

2 red onions, finely sliced

2–3 large garlic cloves, crushed (optional)

1 tablespoon sherry vinegar or white wine vinegar

2 lb. cooked or canned green flageolet beans, white cannellini beans, or a mixture of both

4 handfuls of fresh basil leaves and small sprigs

sea salt and freshly ground black pepper

crusty bread, to serve

*a stove-top grill pan*

**Serves 6 as an appetizer, 4 as an entrée**

If using fresh tuna, brush with olive oil and put into a preheated stove-top grill pan. Cook for 3 minutes on each side or until brown, but still pink in the center (the time depends on the thickness of the fish). Remove from the pan, let cool, and tear into large chunks.

Put the olive oil, onions, garlic, and vinegar into a mixing bowl and beat with a fork. Add the beans and, using a metal spoon, toss until well coated.

Add the tuna and basil, then salt and pepper to taste. Spoon into a serving bowl and serve with crusty bread .

A marvelous, simple chicken salad named after the Gonzagas, who were the Dukes of Mantua, near Modena, the home of balsamic vinegar. True balsamic vinegar is rare and expensive, but you need only a small amount of this rich, sweet dark liquid to transform a dish.

# insalata gonzaga

4 oz. pine nuts

1 lb. skinless, boneless, roasted chicken breasts

⅓ cup extra virgin olive oil

1 tablespoon wine vinegar, red or white

2 small red radicchio lettuces, leaves separated

¼ cup raisins*

1–2 tablespoons balsamic vinegar

sea salt and freshly cracked black pepper

4 oz. fresh Parmesan cheese at room temperature, cut into shards, to serve

**Serves 4**

Put the pine nuts into a dry skillet and heat gently, stirring, until lightly golden. Remove to a plate and set aside.

Slice the chicken or pull it into shreds. Put the olive oil and vinegar into a salad bowl, add a pinch of salt, and beat with a fork. Add the chicken and radicchio to the bowl and toss gently.

Serve on salad plates, sprinkle with the raisins, pepper, and balsamic vinegar, and top with shards of fresh Parmesan.

**\*Note** For this salad, I sometimes put the raisins into a bowl and pour over enough verjuice to cover. Soak for 10 minutes before adding to the salad. Verjuice is halfway between vinegar and wine—delicious, if a little difficult to find. You could also soak the raisins in a mixture of 2 tablespoons wine vinegar and 2–4 tablespoons water.

bread
and
pizza

This quick food processor pizza dough also makes excellent focaccia. Olive oil is used in both the rich, flavorful topping and the dough itself—it is delicious as well as authentic and eminently practical, since there is no need to rub the flour into the fat or oil.

# focaccia
## with olives

1 package active dry yeast, ¼ oz.

1⅔ cups all-purpose flour, plus ¼ cup for shaping

½ teaspoon sea salt flakes

2 tablespoons extra virgin olive oil

**Topping**

finely grated zest and juice of 1 orange

¼ cup extra virgin olive oil

2 garlic cloves, crushed

2 tablespoons fresh rosemary leaves, coarsely chopped

½ teaspoon coarsely crushed black pepper

1 teaspoon sea salt flakes or crystals

6 oz. dry-cured black olives, such as niçoise

*a large baking tray, greased*

**Serves 4**

Put the yeast, flour, and salt into a food processor fitted with a plastic blade. Pulse briefly to sift the ingredients. Mix the oil and ¾ cup warm water in a small bowl and, with the machine running, pour it in all at once through the feed tube. Process, in short bursts, for 15 seconds until a soft mass forms (not a ball). It will be sticky and soft.

Scoop out the dough onto a lightly floured work surface, adding the extra ¼ cup flour as you knead. Roll, pat, and punch down the dough for 2 minutes, then put the ball of dough into an oiled mixing bowl. Enclose the whole bowl in a large plastic bag. Leave in a warm place until the dough has doubled in size, about 50 minutes.

Transfer the risen dough onto a lightly floured work surface, then pat and stretch the dough into a rectangle, about 12 x 9 inches. Transfer to a greased baking tray. Prod the dough all over with your fingertips to form dimples to take the topping.

Put the orange zest and juice, olive oil, crushed garlic, rosemary, black pepper, and half the salt into a bowl and, using a wooden spoon, mix well. Pour the mixture over the dough. Dot with the olives, pushing them well into the dimples. Set aside for 30 minutes to rest the dough.

Bake in a preheated oven at 400°F for 25–30 minutes or until crusty and aromatic. Sprinkle with the remaining salt. Cut into generous squares, then serve hot or warm.

There isn't much to beat warm, freshly baked focaccia. The key to the lovely, soft texture is to cover the bread with a clean dish towel as soon as it comes out of the oven—the steam will prevent a hard crust forming. You can vary the ingredients by adding chopped olives, tiny cubes of cheese, or chopped fresh thyme. Focaccia is best eaten within a day or two of making.

# tomato focaccia

3⅓ cups all-purpose flour, plus extra for dusting

1 teaspoon fine sea salt

1 package active dry yeast, ¼ oz.

3 tablespoons extra virgin olive oil

6 sun-dried tomatoes in oil, drained and chopped

1 cup tepid water

1 teaspoon coarse sea salt

a sprig of fresh rosemary, chopped

2 tablespoons chile oil

*a large baking tray, greased*

**Serves 6**

Put the flour, fine salt, and yeast into a large bowl and mix. Make a well in the center. Add 2 tablespoons of the olive oil, the sun-dried tomatoes, and tepid water to the well, then gradually work in the flour to make a soft dough. Sprinkle with a little flour if the mixture feels too sticky, but make sure it's not dry. The dough should be pliable and smooth.

Transfer the dough to a lightly floured work surface and knead for 10 minutes, sprinkling with flour when needed, until the dough is smooth and stretchy.

Rub some olive oil over the surface and return the dough to the mixing bowl. Cover with a clean dish towel and set aside for about 1 hour, until the mixture has doubled in size.

Transfer the risen dough to a lightly floured surface and knead for 2 minutes, until the excess air is knocked out. Roll out the dough to make an oval, about 12 inches long. Carefully set on the prepared baking tray and cover with a clean dish towel. Set aside for 30 minutes or until almost doubled in size.

Prod the dough all over with your fingertips to form dimples. Sprinkle with the remaining tablespoon of olive oil, salt, and rosemary. Bake in a preheated oven at 400°F for about 20–25 minutes until risen and golden.

Remove the focaccia from the oven, cover with a clean cloth, and set aside on a wire rack for at least 15 minutes to cool. Drizzle with the chile oil. Serve warm or at room temperature.

There is nothing better than homemade pizza and once you have tried it you will never want to buy ready-made again. You can also add flavorings such as chopped herbs or cheese to the dough.

# basic
# pizza dough

1²⁄₃ cups all-purpose flour, plus extra for sprinkling

½ teaspoon fine sea salt

1 package active dry yeast, ¼ oz.

2 tablespoons extra virgin olive oil

½ cup tepid water

**Makes 1**

**1** Put the flour, salt, and yeast into a large bowl and mix.

**2** Make a well in the center and add the olive oil and water. Gradually work in the flour to make a soft dough. Sprinkle over a little flour if the mixture feels too sticky, but make sure it is not too dry. The dough should be pliable and smooth.

**3** Transfer the dough to a lightly floured work surface and knead for 10 minutes, sprinkling with flour when needed, until the dough is smooth and stretchy. Rub some olive oil over the surface and return the dough to the mixing bowl. Cover with a clean dish towel and set aside for 1 hour, until the dough has doubled in size.

**4** Transfer the risen dough onto a lightly floured work surface and knead for 2 minutes, until the excess air is knocked out. Roll out the dough according to the recipe you are following.

**Variation**

**Polenta dough** To make a polenta base, use ⅓ cup instant polenta or fine cornmeal and 1⅓ cups all-purpose flour.

**Note** If you are in a real hurry, there are some good quality package dough mixes available. Follow the instructions on the package, but remember to roll it out very thinly.

Roasting peppers is a delicious way to bring out their sweetness. Make sure they are still warm when you add them to the dressing, so they absorb all the flavors of the garlic and parsley.

# roasted pepper pizza

2 red bell peppers

2 yellow bell peppers

2 garlic cloves, finely chopped

a small bunch of flat-leaf parsley, finely chopped

2 tablespoons olive oil

1 recipe pizza dough (page 38)

all-purpose flour, for dusting

1 recipe tomato sauce (page 72)

6 oz. tomatoes, sliced or halved

6 oz. fresh mozzarella cheese, drained and sliced

sea salt and freshly ground black pepper

*a large baking tray or pizza baking stone*

**Makes 1**

Put a large baking tray or pizza stone into the oven at 425°F to heat. Put the peppers into a small roasting pan and bake in the preheated oven for 30 minutes, turning them occasionally, until the skins blacken and blister.

Meanwhile, put the garlic and parsley into a small mixing bowl. Add the olive oil, then add salt and pepper to taste.

Remove the peppers from the oven, cover with a clean dish towel, and set aside for 10 minutes or until cool enough to handle but still warm. Pierce the base of each pepper and squeeze the juices into the parsley and oil mixture. Peel and seed the peppers. Cut the flesh into 1-inch strips and add to the mixture. Cover and set aside at room temperature until needed.

Transfer the pizza dough to a lightly floured work surface and roll out to 12 inches diameter. Brush with a little olive oil, then spoon over the tomato sauce and arrange the tomatoes and mozzarella cheese on top. Spoon the pepper mixture over the top.

Carefully set the pizza onto the hot baking sheet or pizza stone and bake in the preheated oven for about 20–25 minutes until crisp and golden. Using a sharp knife or pizza cutter, cut into wedges and serve.

Bresaola—dried lean beef from the Alpine region of Italy—has a lovely sweetness, which here complements the peppery arugula and salty Parmesan. If you can't find bresaola, use a dry-cured ham, such prosciutto, instead.

# eggplant pizza
## with bresaola, arugula, and parmesan

1 eggplant, cut into ½-inch slices

¼ cup olive oil, plus extra to serve

1 recipe pizza dough (page 38)

all-purpose flour, for dusting

1 recipe tomato sauce (page 72)

3 oz. very finely sliced bresaola or prosciutto

a large handful of arugula, sliced if large

Parmesan cheese, freshly grated or shaved

sea salt and freshly ground black pepper

a large baking tray or pizza baking stone

a stove-top grill pan

**Makes 1**

Put a large baking tray or pizza stone into the oven at 400°F to heat. Brush the eggplant slices with the olive oil and sprinkle salt and pepper lightly on both sides. Preheat a stove-top grill pan or large nonstick skillet over medium heat, add the eggplant, and cook for 3–4 minutes on each side until tender and charred with marks.

Transfer the dough to a lightly floured work surface and roll out to 12 inches diameter. Brush with a little olive oil, then spoon over the tomato sauce and arrange the eggplant slices on top.

Carefully set the pizza onto the hot baking tray or pizza stone and bake in the preheated oven for 15 minutes. Remove from the oven and ripple the bresaola or prosciutto evenly across the pizza. Return the pizza to the oven and bake for a further 5–10 minutes until crisp and golden.

Sprinkle with arugula and Parmesan cheese. Top with a splash of olive oil and a good grinding of black pepper. Using a sharp knife or pizza cutter, cut into wedges and serve.

The pizza for people who just can't make up their minds which one to choose. If you can't find artichokes, use roasted peppers or char-grilled eggplant instead.

# quattro stagioni

¼ cup olive oil

1 shallot, finely sliced

6 oz. mushrooms, sliced

2 tablespoons chopped fresh flat-leaf parsley

1 recipe pizza dough (page 38)

all-purpose flour, for dusting

1 recipe tomato sauce (page 72)

2 oz. prosciutto, shredded

6 black olives, such as niçoise

4 artichoke hearts in brine or oil, drained and quartered

3 oz. mozzarella cheese, drained and sliced

4 anchovy fillets in oil, drained

sea salt and freshly ground black pepper

fresh basil leaves, to serve

*a large baking tray or pizza baking stone*

**Makes 1**

Put a large baking tray or pizza stone into the oven at 400°F to heat. Heat 2 tablespoons of the oil in a nonstick skillet, add the shallot, and cook for 2 minutes. Add the mushrooms and cook for a further 2–3 minutes until softened and golden. Stir in the parsley, then add salt and pepper to taste.

Turn out the pizza dough onto a lightly floured work surface and roll out to 12 inches diameter. Brush with a little olive oil, then spoon over the tomato sauce. Pile the mushrooms over one-quarter of the pizza. Arrange the prosciutto and olives on another quarter, and the artichoke hearts on a third section. Arrange the mozzarella on the remaining section and put the anchovies on top.

Sprinkle a little more olive oil, salt, and plenty of black pepper over the whole pizza. Carefully set the pizza onto the hot baking tray or pizza stone and bake in the preheated oven for 20–25 minutes until crisp and golden. Using a sharp knife or pizza cutter, cut into quarters, sprinkle the basil over the artichoke portion, and serve.

Cooking a pizza upside down is a great way to make sure you get a crisp crust. It also keeps all those sweet tomato juices from escaping—the result is truly spectacular.

# topsy turvy
# cherry tomato pizza

2–3 tablespoons olive oil

4 oz. prosciutto or bacon, chopped

2¼ lb. cherry tomatoes

1 recipe pizza dough (page 38)

all-purpose flour, for dusting

juice of ½ lemon

2 teaspoons chopped fresh mint

sea salt and freshly ground black pepper

*a jelly roll pan or baking tray, about 14 x 10 inches*

**Makes 1**

Heat 1 tablespoon of the oil in a large, nonstick skillet. Add the prosciutto or bacon pieces and cook for 2–3 minutes until golden.

Transfer the prosciutto or bacon and the pan oil to a jelly roll pan or baking tray. Put the cherry tomatoes into the pan, making sure that they fit in a single layer. Sprinkle with salt and black pepper.

Transfer the dough onto a lightly floured work surface and roll out to about the same size as the pan. Put the dough on top of the tomatoes, tucking any overlap inside the pan. Bake in a preheated oven at 400°F for about 20–25 minutes until the crust is crisp and dark golden.

Meanwhile, put the lemon juice, mint, and remaining olive oil into a bowl and, using a metal spoon, mix until blended.

Carefully invert the pizza onto a chopping board. Drizzle the lemon and mint mixture over the top, then, using a sharp knife, cut into slices and serve warm.

The combination of rosemary, prosciutto, and soft goat cheese makes a fragrant, summery pizza. This is just as good served at room temperature with a leafy salad—ideal picnic food.

# goat cheese pizza
## with prosciutto and rosemary

1 recipe pizza dough (page 38)

all-purpose flour, for dusting

2 tablespoons olive oil

8 oz. soft goat cheese

2 teaspoons coarsely chopped fresh rosemary

4 oz. prosciutto, chopped

sea salt and freshly ground black pepper

*a large baking tray or pizza baking stone*

**Makes 1**

Put a large baking tray or pizza stone into the oven at 400°F to heat. Transfer the dough onto a lightly floured surface and roll out to 12 inches diameter. Brush with 1 tablespoon of the olive oil, then crumble over the cheese and top with the rosemary and prosciutto.

Sprinkle the pizza with the remaining tablespoon of oil, salt, and plenty of black pepper. Carefully set the pizza on the hot baking tray or pizza stone and bake in the preheated oven for 20–25 minutes until crisp and golden. Using a sharp knife or pizza cutter, cut into wedges and serve warm, or at room temperature.

A light and crispy pizza with a rather delicate flavour. For a non-vegetarian version, add some prosciutto, bacon, or pancetta with the cheese.

# wafer potato pizza
## with taleggio

1 recipe pizza dough (page 38)

all-purpose flour, for dusting

2 tablespoons olive oil

12 oz. red-skinned potatoes

6 sage leaves, finely shredded

2 garlic cloves, crushed

7 oz. Taleggio cheese, cut into small pieces

sea salt and freshly ground black pepper

*a large baking tray or pizza baking stone*

**Serves 4**

Put the baking tray or pizza stone into the oven at 400°F to heat.

Divide the dough into 4 pieces and, on a lightly floured work surface, roll each one into a wafer-thin oval, about 11 inches long. Brush the dough with 1 tablespoon of the olive oil.

Using a mandoline or food processor, cut the potatoes into wafer-thin slices. Put the slices into a mixing bowl, add the sage, garlic, and remaining tablespoon of olive oil, and, using a metal spoon, toss to coat. Put a single layer of potato slices over each dough base and sprinkle with salt and plenty of black pepper.

Carefully set the pizzas on the hot baking tray or pizza stone and bake in the preheated oven for 10 minutes. Remove from the oven and dot with the Taleggio cheese. Return to the oven and bake for a further 5–10 minutes until crisp and golden. Serve hot or warm.

The secret of a delicious pizza marinara is the tomatoes. Choose really ripe, plump specimens. It's well worth the extra effort of peeling and seeding them—the result is a satin-smooth, fragrant, and fruity sauce. Don't be tempted to add any cheese!

# pizza marinara

3–4 tablespoons olive oil

1½ lb. ripe tomatoes, peeled, seeded, and chopped

1 recipe pizza dough (page 38)

all-purpose flour, for dusting

3 garlic cloves, very finely sliced

1 tablespoon chopped fresh oregano or marjoram

sea salt and freshly ground black pepper

*a large baking tray or pizza baking stone*

**Makes 1**

Put the baking sheet or pizza stone into a preheated oven at 425°F to heat.

Heat 2 tablespoons of the oil in a saucepan and add the tomatoes, then salt and pepper to taste. Cook for about 5 minutes, stirring occasionally, until thickened and pulpy.

Turn out the pizza dough onto a lightly floured work surface and roll out to 12 inches diameter. Brush with a little olive oil. Spoon over the tomato sauce and sprinkle with the garlic, oregano, and a little more olive oil.

Carefully set the pizza on the hot baking tray or pizza stone and bake in the preheated oven for 15–20 minutes or until crisp and golden. Serve hot or at room temperature.

Mushrooms are always an excellent choice for pizza toppings. For a range of flavor and texture, use a mixture of varieties, including regular, shiitake, and portobello. The basil, chile, and garlic oil isn't essential, but adds quite a boost to the pizza. Some food stores stock a variety of infused oils, such as basil or lemon oil, and these would make a good substitute.

# mushroom pizza
## with basil, chile, and garlic oil

1 recipe pizza dough (page 38)

all-purpose flour, for dusting

½ cup olive oil

1 recipe tomato sauce (page 72)

14 oz. mixed mushrooms, thickly sliced

6 oz. fresh mozzarella cheese, drained and chopped

2 larger garlic cloves, halved

1 large, mild, red fresh chile, seeded and quartered

8 fresh basil leaves, finely shredded

sea salt and freshly ground black pepper

*a large baking tray or pizza baking stone*

**Makes 1**

Put the baking tray or pizza stone into the oven at 425°F to heat. Transfer the pizza dough onto a lightly floured work surface and roll out to 12 inches diameter. Brush with a little olive oil, then spoon over the tomato sauce and add the mushrooms and mozzarella.

Sprinkle the pizza with a little olive oil, salt, and pepper. Carefully set the pizza onto the hot baking tray or pizza stone and bake in the preheated oven for 20–25 minutes until crisp and golden.

Meanwhile, put the remaining olive oil into a small saucepan and add the garlic and chile. Heat very gently for 10 minutes until the garlic is softened and translucent. Remove from the heat and let cool slightly for 5 minutes.

Using a fork, remove and discard the garlic and chile. Stir the basil into the flavored oil and drizzle over the hot pizza. Using a sharp knife or pizza cutter, cut into wedges and serve hot or warm.

Whatever kind of cabbage you choose for this soup, make sure you don't cook it any longer than 7–8 minutes. Cabbage doesn't like it, and will punish you with a dreadful stink. Cavolo nero is a dark and delicious Italian variety with white stalks and puckered leaves.

# pumpkin bean soup

4 red bell peppers, halved and seeded

¼ cup olive oil

4 onions, finely sliced

3 garlic cloves, crushed

3 lb. pumpkin or butternut squash, peeled, seeded, and cut into 1-inch cubes or wedges

1½ cups chicken stock

6 oz. cavolo nero or other cabbage, cut into 2-inch pieces

2 cans cannellini beans, about 14 oz. each, rinsed and drained

sea salt and freshly ground black pepper

fresh Parmesan cheese, cut in long shavings, to serve (optional)

**Serves 4**

Arrange the peppers on a broiler rack, skin side up, and cook under the preheated hot broiler until the skins blacken and blister. Transfer to a small saucepan, cover with a lid, and let stand for about 5–10 minutes to steam off the skins. Remove from the saucepan and scrape off and discard the skins. Cut each half into 3 pieces and set aside.

Heat the oil in a large, heavy saucepan. Add the onions and sauté gently until softened and translucent. Add the garlic and sauté until golden. Add the pumpkin, toss to coat with the oil, and sauté until lightly browned.

Add the stock and bring to a boil. Add the cavolo nero or other cabbage and the reserved peppers, return to a boil, then simmer for about 6 minutes. Stir in the beans, then add salt and black pepper to taste and heat until bubbling. Serve sprinkled with shavings of fresh Parmesan.

Two classic Tuscan soups for the price of one—serve the day it's made, or the next day after reboiling—"ribollita." The garlic toast isn't traditional, but helps the soup serve more people. The lettuce added at the end isn't traditional either, but adds an extra crunch.

# tuscan ribollita

8 oz. dried cannellini beans, about 1½ cups

2 medium onions (1 cut into 4 wedges through the root, and 1 sliced)

3 carrots (1 cut into quarters lengthwise, and 2 sliced)

6 garlic cloves, crushed

⅓ cup extra virgin olive oil, plus extra for serving

1 fresh red chile, seeded and sliced

8 oz. tomatoes, peeled and chopped, about 2 small or 1 large

1 leek, split and well cleaned under running water, then sliced

2 celery stalks, finely chopped

2 sprigs of fresh thyme

3 salad potatoes, cut into big pieces

1 Savoy cabbage or cavolo nero, sliced

sea salt and freshly ground black pepper

**Garlic toast (optional)**

4 tablespoons unsalted butter, mashed with 1 crushed garlic clove

8 slices ciabatta bread, toasted

1 romaine lettuce, sliced

¼ cup chopped fresh flat-leaf parsley

**Serves 4–6**

Put the beans into a large bowl and cover with cold water. Soak for 4 hours or overnight. Drain thoroughly, then put the beans into a heavy saucepan with the onion wedges, quartered carrot, and half the garlic. Cover with water, bring to a boil, and simmer until done (the time will depend on the age of the beans, but about 1 hour).

Drain the beans into a large measuring cup, reserving the liquid. Make up to 6 cups with water. Remove the flavorings from the beans, then put half the beans into a food processor and process to a coarse purée. Press the purée through a strainer or potato ricer to remove any bits of bean skin.

Put about ¼ cup of the olive oil into a large saucepan, add the sliced onion, and cook until softened and translucent. Add the chile and remaining garlic and cook for a further 5 minutes. Add the tomatoes and puréed beans, then season with salt and pepper. Cook for about 5 minutes, then add the remaining carrots, leek, celery, thyme, potatoes, and cabbage. Add the 6 cups reserved liquid, bring to a boil, and simmer until the vegetables are done, about 20 minutes.

Add the whole beans, then add salt and pepper to taste. Reheat gently and serve immediately or set aside until the next day to make ribollita.

To serve as ribollita, reheat gently, then serve. If you would like to make the soup go further, make garlic toast—spread the garlic butter over the toast and put into 4 large soup bowls. Add the lettuce, ladle the soup over the top, and drizzle with olive oil. Sprinkle with chopped fresh parsley and serve.

*Zucca* is Italian for pumpkin. In Italy, the most common variety is a large squashed globe with a dusty orange skin. Butternut squash makes an acceptable substitute. Even better are those with greenish-blue or gray skins—the flesh is denser, sweeter, and less watery. In Italy, the soup is made without potatoes, but they do thicken the soup nicely and smooth the strong, very sweet taste of pumpkin. The milk is important—pumpkin loves milk—and it's also very fond of nutmeg.

# zuppa di zucca

2 lb. pumpkin or butternut squash, peeled, seeded, and cut into large chunks

2 large potatoes, quartered

1 quart boiling chicken stock or water

4 tablespoons unsalted butter

2 tablespoons olive oil

2 large onions, finely sliced

1 cup milk

sea salt

**To serve**

¼ cup sour cream

freshly grated nutmeg

pumpkin chips (page 90)

**Serves 4**

Put the pumpkin and potatoes into a large saucepan, add chicken stock or 1 quart boiling water to cover, then simmer until tender. Drain, reserving the cooking liquid.

Heat the butter and olive oil in a large, nonstick skillet, add the onions, and sauté until softened and lightly golden. Transfer to a food processor or blender, then add the pumpkin and potatoes, in batches if necessary. Blend, adding enough milk and cooking liquid to make a thick purée.

Transfer the purée to the saucepan and stir in enough stock to make a thick, creamy soup. Add salt to taste and reheat gently. Ladle the soup into 4 warmed soup bowls, top with sour cream, nutmeg, and a few pumpkin chips, then serve.

**Variation**

**Roasted pumpkin soup** For a smoky taste, instead of boiling the pumpkin, roast it in a preheated oven at 425°F for about 30–40 minutes until tender.

True minestrone is a thick soup made of chunky vegetables and borlotti beans and either small pasta shapes or rice (especially in the north)—a typical recipe is given below. In summer, the rice-thickened soup can be chilled, like an Italian version of gazpacho. This is a lighter version of the classic soup—more like a broth.

# summer minestrone

2 oz. small dried pasta shapes, about ½ cup

1 tablespoon olive oil

1 red onion, chopped

1 garlic clove, finely chopped

2 celery stalks, finely sliced

6 oz. baby carrots, finely sliced

2 plum tomatoes, coarsely chopped

5 cups vegetable stock

6 oz. string beans, finely sliced

2 tablespoons Classic Basil Pesto (page 71)

salt and freshly ground black pepper

freshly grated Parmesan cheese, to serve

**Serves 4**

Bring a large saucepan of water to a boil. Add a good pinch of salt, then add the pasta and cook until *al dente* or according to the instructions on the package. Drain well.

Meanwhile, heat the olive oil in another large saucepan, add the onion and garlic, and cook gently for 3 minutes. Add the celery and carrots and cook for a further 2 minutes. Add the tomatoes and cook for a further 2 minutes.

Add the stock and beans, bring to a boil, then simmer for 5–10 minutes until the vegetables are cooked and tender.

Add the drained pasta, stir in the pesto, then add salt and pepper. Ladle the soup into 4 large, warmed soup bowls, sprinkle with freshly grated Parmesan, and serve.

**Classic minestrone** Use the same vegetables as in the main recipe, but cut them into large chunks, peeling the tomatoes first. Heat 2 tablespoons olive oil or butter in a large saucepan, add 4 oz. sliced prosciutto, the onion, and garlic, and sauté until golden. Add the celery and carrots and sauté until lightly browned. Add 1 lb. cooked or canned pinto beans, the runner beans, and 2 baking potatoes, cut into chunks. Add 5 cups chicken or vegetable stock, the tomatoes, and 1 cup shelled peas, fresh or frozen. Bring to a boil, cover, and simmer for 2 hours, adding 2 cups tiny pasta shapes or rice for the last 10 minutes. Serve sprinkled with chopped parsley.

A few dried porcini mushrooms will give a stronger flavor to a soup made with ordinary cultivated mushrooms. Use large, open field mushrooms (portobellos) to give a deeper color.

# mushroom soup
## with porcini and parsley

1 oz. dried porcini mushrooms

¼ cup olive oil

6 large portobello mushrooms, wiped, trimmed, and sliced

1 onion, halved and finely sliced

3 garlic cloves, crushed

a pinch of freshly grated nutmeg

leaves from a large bunch of fresh flat-leaf parsley, finely chopped in a food processor

5 cups boiling chicken stock

4 tablespoons unsalted butter

¼ cup all-purpose flour

sea salt and freshly ground black pepper

1 fresh porcini, sliced and sautéed, to serve (optional)

**To serve**

½ cup coarsely chopped fresh flat-leaf parsley

½ cup sour cream

**Serves 4–6**

Put the dried porcini into a mixing bowl, add 1 cup boiling water, and let soak for 15 minutes. Heat the olive oil in a large, nonstick skillet, add the fresh mushrooms, and sauté gently until browned but still firm.

Add the onion to the skillet and sauté until softened, then add the garlic, nutmeg, and parsley. Rinse any grit out of the porcini and strain their soaking liquid several times through cheesecloth to remove any grit. Add the liquid and porcini to the pan (reserve a few small ones for garnish) and bring to the boil.

Reserve a few of the sautéed mushrooms for serving and transfer the remaining mushroom mixture to a blender. Add 2 ladles of the boiling chicken stock, then blend to a purée.

Heat the butter in a large saucepan, stir in the flour, and cook gently, stirring constantly, until the mixture is very dark brown (take care or it will burn). Add the remaining stock, 1 ladle at a time, stirring well after each addition. Add the mushroom mixture, bring to a boil, then simmer for 20 minutes and add salt and pepper to taste. Ladle the soup into warmed soup bowls and serve topped with a few reserved mushrooms or porcini, coarsely chopped parsley, and a spoonful of sour cream.

There's something really satisfying about making pasta at home. A food processor and pasta-rolling machine make light work of the job, but you can easily make and roll the dough by hand. You can cut the rolled pasta into strips or use it to make these subtly flavored ravioli.

# fresh filled pasta

2 cups all-purpose flour, plus extra for kneading and rolling

salt

3 medium eggs

**Pumpkin filling**

1 lb. pumpkin or butternut squash, peeled, seeded, and cut into 2-inch pieces

2 shallots, chopped

4 sage leaves, chopped, plus sprigs to serve

1/3 cup dried bread crumbs

1 cup freshly grated Parmesan cheese

1/4 teaspoon freshly grated nutmeg

1 egg

6 tablespoons butter, melted

sea salt and freshly ground black pepper

*a pasta machine*

**Makes 1 lb. dough
Serves 4**

**1** Put the flour and a pinch of salt into a food processor, then add the eggs. Process in short bursts until the mixture forms sticky crumbs. Alternatively, to make the dough by hand, sift the flour into a large bowl, sprinkle with salt, and make a well in the center. Add the eggs to the well and, using your hands, gradually work the flour into the eggs. Transfer the mixture to a lightly floured work surface and bring together with your hands to form a soft dough. Knead the dough for 5 minutes until it feels smooth, then wrap in plastic and chill in the refrigerator for 30 minutes.

**2** Divide the pasta dough into 4 pieces. Roll each piece through the pasta machine, going down a setting each time, and dusting with flour when necessary. Alternatively, transfer the dough to a lightly floured work surface and roll out to 1/8-inch thick.

**3** To make ravioli, put a sheet of rolled pasta dough onto a lightly floured work surface. Put tablespoons of the filling* in evenly spaced mounds on the dough, leaving about 2 inches between each mound. Cover with a second sheet of rolled pasta dough and, using your fingers, press firmly around the mounds to seal. Using a pasta cutter or sharp knife, cut lines between the mounds to make separate squares, about 3 inches each. Repeat with the remaining dough and filling to make 20 ravioli squares.

**4** Bring a large saucepan of water to a boil. Add a good pinch of salt, then add the ravioli and cook for 3–4 minutes until they rise to the surface and are cooked through. Using a slotted spoon, drain carefully and return to the pan. Spoon over melted butter, sprinkle with freshly grated Parmesan, then serve.

**Note** For filled pasta, use each sheet immediately after rolling, or the pasta will dry out. For ribbons or shapes, let the sheets dry out on a clean cloth for 30 minutes before cutting.

**\*Filling** To make the filling, simmer the pumpkin, shallots, and chopped sage in salted water for 8 minutes. Drain, then mash. Stir in the breadcrumbs, cheese, and nutmeg. Divide into 16–20 portions.

Pesto is native to Liguria on the Mediterranean coast of northwest Italy. Ligurian basil is said to be more aromatic than any other—but good pesto can also be made with parsley, arugula, or sun-dried tomatoes. Most pesto includes nuts, usually pine nuts, but occasionally walnuts. It makes a superb, fragrant sauce for pasta, and a spoonful or two is a delicious addition to a vegetable soup.

# classic
# basil pesto

2 tablespoons pine nuts

2 oz. fresh basil leaves, about 2½ cups

2 garlic cloves

2 tablespoons olive oil

4 tablespoons unsalted butter, softened

2 oz. freshly grated Parmesan cheese

freshly ground black pepper

Serves 4

Put the pine nuts into a small, dry skillet and cook until golden. Let cool.

Put the basil, pine nuts, and garlic into a food processor and process until finely chopped. Alternatively, use a mortar and pestle. Add the olive oil, butter, Parmesan, and black pepper to taste. Process briefly until blended.

Serve immediately, or transfer to an airtight container or cover with plastic wrap and refrigerate for up to 4 days.

**Variations**

**Parsley pesto**  Use fresh flat-leaf parsley instead of basil and almonds instead of pine nuts.

**Arugula pesto**  Use half arugula and half fresh basil, which gives a bitter edge but tastes curiously good.

This simple sauce is perfect for pasta or as a basic topping for almost any pizza. Choose cans of whole plum tomatoes rather than the chopped sort, which can have a bitter edge. Cook the sauce for at least thirty minutes to give it time to develop some richness. Alternatively, add a pinch of hot red pepper flakes to give the sauce an extra kick.

## classic
# tomato sauce

1 tablespoon olive oil

1 shallot, finely chopped

2 garlic cloves, finely chopped

1 can whole plum tomatoes, about 14 oz.

a sprig of fresh rosemary or thyme, or a pinch of dried oregano

a pinch of sugar

sea salt and freshly ground black pepper

**Serves 4**

Heat the olive oil in a small saucepan, add the shallot and garlic, and cook for 3–4 minutes until softened. Add the tomatoes, breaking them up briefly with a wooden spoon. Add the herbs, sugar, salt, and pepper.

Bring the mixture to a boil and partly cover with a lid. Reduce the heat and simmer very gently for 30–60 minutes, stirring from time to time and breaking up the tomatoes with the back of the wooden spoon, until the sauce turns dark red and small droplets of oil appear on the surface.

Discard any woody herb sprigs. Add salt and pepper, if necessary, then let cool slightly before using.

**Variation**

**Fiery tomato sauce** Put 14 oz. canned passata or puréed tomatoes, 2 tablespoons olive oil, 2 chopped garlic cloves, 6 torn fresh basil leaves, a pinch of hot red pepper flakes, and ¼ teaspoon sugar into a small saucepan, with salt and pepper to taste. Proceed as in the main recipe.

One of those simple pantry dishes that saves your life when you get home late, tired, and hungry. With just four basic ingredients, you can always make this at very short notice.

# white spaghetti

6 oz. dried pasta,
such as spaghetti

1/3 cup olive oil

4 garlic cloves,
halved

6 anchovy fillets
in oil, drained

sea salt and freshly
ground black pepper

**Serves 2**

Bring a large saucepan of water to a boil. Add a good pinch of salt, then add the pasta and cook until *al dente* or according to the directions on the package.

Put the olive oil and garlic into a small saucepan and heat very gently over a low heat for 4–5 minutes until the garlic is pale gold but not browned. Remove and discard the garlic.

Add the anchovies and 1/2 cup water to the saucepan and simmer rapidly, beating with a fork until the anchovies have almost dissolved. Add pepper and a tiny pinch of salt.

Drain the pasta and return it to the warmed saucepan, then add the anchovy mixture. Using 2 forks, toss well to cover with the sauce. Spoon the pasta into 2 large serving bowls or plates and serve.

A wonderful combination of two very rich pasta sauces—and absolutely delicious! Make your own fresh pasta from this recipe or the one on page 69, otherwise buy fresh or dried pasta and cook according to the directions on the package.

# fettuccine
## with gorgonzola sauce and pesto

**Fresh rich pasta dough**
1²⁄₃ cups all-purpose flour
2 eggs
2 egg yolks
a pinch of sea salt

**Gorgonzola sauce**
4 oz. Gorgonzola or dolcelatte cheese, chopped
½ cup milk
¼ cup heavy cream
2 tablespoons unsalted butter

**To serve**
¼ cup Classic Pesto Sauce (page 71) or store-bought
sprigs of basil
shavings of fresh Parmesan cheese
sea salt and cracked black pepper

*a pasta machine*

**Serves 4**

Put all the ingredients for the pasta dough into a food processor and process to a dough. Turn out the dough onto a lightly floured work surface and knead until the dough comes together. Roll it through a pasta machine according to the manufacturer's instructions. Cut with the fettuccine attachment.

To make the sauce, put the cheese into a small saucepan and melt with the milk, cream, and butter. Cook, stirring constantly, until the sauce has thickened, about 5 minutes.*

Bring a large saucepan of water to a boil. Add a good pinch of salt, then add the pasta and cook until it rises to the surface, about 1–2 minutes. If you are using dried pasta, cook until *al dente* or according to the directions on the package. Drain, then return the pasta to the saucepan, spoon the Gorgonzola sauce over the top, and toss gently. Transfer to 4 large, warmed serving bowls, then add the pesto, Parmesan shavings, and a sprig of basil. Serve with extra Parmesan, some cracked pepper, and a small dish of sea salt.

**\*Note** The pesto can be stirred into the sauce at this point, or spooned on top of the pasta just before serving.

The clams are the real stars of this dish, but it's crucial that the sauce is smooth. If you only have canned tomatoes, purée them in a blender before using. Delicious as this is, it's not an elegant meal to eat, so be prepared: you'll be using your fingers to pick the clams from their shells. Provide guests with fingerbowls of warm water and a slice of lemon.

# pasta con le vongole

2 tablespoons olive oil

2 garlic cloves, finely chopped

a sprig of fresh rosemary

2 cups puréed tomato

½ teaspoon sugar

2 lb. fresh baby clams in shells

10 oz. dried pasta, such as spaghetti or linguine

2 tablespoons chopped fresh flat-leaf parsley

salt and freshly ground black pepper

**Serves 4**

Heat the oil in a saucepan, add the garlic and rosemary, and cook over low heat for 2 minutes. Add the tomatoes, sugar, salt, and pepper. Bring to a boil, cover with a lid, and simmer for 30 minutes. Remove and discard the rosemary.

Put the clams and 2 tablespoons of water into a large saucepan. Cover with a lid and cook over medium heat for 4–5 minutes, shaking the pan occasionally until all the shells have opened. Discard any that remain closed. Let cool.

Bring a large saucepan of water to a boil. Add a pinch of salt, then add the pasta, and cook until *al dente* or according to the directions on the package.

Strain the clam cooking juices through a cheesecloth into a measuring cup, leaving behind any grit. Add the juices to the tomato sauce. Shell half the clams and discard the empty shells. Add the shelled and unshelled clams to the tomato sauce and simmer for 3–4 minutes.

Drain the pasta and return it to the warmed saucepan. Add the clams and chopped parsley and, using 2 forks, toss gently. Spoon the pasta into 4 warmed serving bowls and serve.

This hearty soup of pasta and beans is a classic from the region of Puglia in Italy—the pasta shapes traditionally used are orecchiette, meaning "little ears." Try using different pasta shapes, such as fusilli or rotelle if you can't find orecchiette.

# pasta e fagioli

2 tablespoons olive oil

1 small onion, finely chopped

2 garlic cloves, finely chopped

1 potato, chopped

2 ripe tomatoes, coarsely chopped

5 cups chicken or vegetable stock

a sprig of fresh thyme, sage, or rosemary

2 cans cannellini beans, drained, about 14 oz. each

6 oz. small dried pasta shapes, such as orecchiette, about 1½ cups

a pinch of hot red pepper flakes

sea salt and freshly ground black pepper

freshly grated Parmesan cheese, to serve

**Serves 4**

Heat the olive oil in a large saucepan, add the onion, garlic, and potato and cook for 3–4 minutes until golden. Add the tomatoes and cook for 2–3 minutes until softened.

Add the stock, a herb sprig, the beans, pasta, pepper flakes, salt, and pepper. Bring to a boil and simmer for about 10 minutes until the pasta and potatoes are cooked.

Ladle the soup into 4 large, warmed soup bowls and serve sprinkled with Parmesan.

**Variations**

Use fresh shelled fava beans instead of the cannellini beans.

Substitute 1 fresh red chile, finely chopped, for the hot red pepper flakes.

Use different pasta shapes, such as fusilli, rotelle, or conchiglie or use small soup pasta, such as anellini or ditali.

An ever-popular Italian dish—perfect for any occasion from an informal gathering to a special dinner party. Serve the lasagne with a crisp salad and crusty bread.

# baked lasagne

1 lb. dried lasagne

10 oz. fresh mozzarella cheese, drained and chopped

1/4 cup freshly grated Parmesan cheese

salt and freshly ground black pepper

**Bolognese sauce**

1/2 oz. dried porcini mushrooms, rinsed

1 tablespoon olive oil

1 onion, finely chopped

1 lb. ground beef

2 oz. prosciutto, chopped

1/2 cup Marsala wine or dry sherry

3 cups puréed tomatoes

**White sauce**

1 quart milk

1 small garlic clove

4 tablespoons unsalted butter

1/3 cup all-purpose flour

*a baking dish, about 12 x 8 x 3 inches, lightly oiled*

**Serves 8**

To make the bolognese sauce, put the dried porcini into a bowl, cover with boiling water, and let soak for 20 minutes until softened. Heat the olive oil in a large saucepan, add the onion, and cook for 2 minutes. Add the ground beef and prosciutto and cook for 3–4 minutes, stirring constantly, until evenly browned. Drain the porcini and discard the soaking water. Chop the porcini, then add to the pan with the Marsala and tomatoes. Cover with a lid and simmer for 1 hour, stirring occasionally, until rich and dark. Add salt and black pepper to taste.

Bring a large saucepan of water to a boil. Add a good pinch of salt, then add the lasagne sheets, one at a time, so that they don't stick together. Cook for 5 minutes, then drain and transfer the lasagne into a bowl of cold water. Drain again and pat dry with paper towels.

To make the white sauce, put the milk and garlic into a small saucepan and heat gently until warm. Melt the butter in a separate saucepan, then stir in the flour and cook for 1 minute. Gradually add the warm milk, stirring constantly to make a smooth sauce. Bring to a boil, then simmer for 2–3 minutes. Remove and discard the garlic clove. Add salt and pepper to taste.

Put 3–4 tablespoons of the bolognese sauce into the baking dish, spread evenly across the base of the dish with a spoon, then cover with a layer of lasagne. Spoon over some white sauce and a few pieces of mozzarella and continue adding layers, starting with another layer of bolognese sauce and finishing with the white sauce and mozzarella, until all the ingredients have been used. Sprinkle with black pepper and freshly grated Parmesan, then bake in a preheated oven at 375°F for about 30 minutes until the top is crusty and golden.

There are a number of different kinds of gnocchi, or dumplings. These, made with cooked mashed potato, are the most common. Others are made with semolina (page 85), pumpkin, or leftover rice. All are incomparable.

# gnocchi
## with tomato sauce

2 lb. large baking potatoes, peeled and cut into large pieces

a pinch of sea salt

2 egg yolks

1⅓ cups all-purpose flour, plus extra for rolling

1 quart boiling water, or beef or chicken stock, for poaching

**To serve**

2–3 cups hot Classic Tomato Sauce (page 72)

a handful of fresh basil leaves

1 tablespoon chopped fresh chives

freshly grated Parmesan cheese (optional)

sea salt and freshly ground black pepper

**Serves 4–8**

To make the gnocchi, bring a large saucepan of lightly salted water to a boil. Add the potatoes and cook until soft. Drain and either mash with a fork or press through a potato ricer into a large mixing bowl. Add the salt and, using a fork, beat the egg yolks and flour into the potatoes, a little at a time, to form a smooth, slightly sticky dough.

Turn out the dough onto a well floured board and roll out into cylinders, about ½-inch diameter. Cut each piece into sections, about 1 inch long. Place each piece on the back of a fork, press down with your thumb, and roll or flick the piece off the end of the fork onto the floured board, leaving grooves on one side of the gnocchi—the grooves will help hold the sauce.

Pour the boiling water or stock into a large saucepan, return to a boil, add the gnocchi about 20 at a time, and cook until they rise to the surface. Simmer for a further 50–60 seconds until cooked through, then, using a slotted spoon, transfer to a large bowl. Repeat until all the gnocchi are cooked.

To serve, spoon a pool of the tomato sauce into 4 wide soup bowls, then add the gnocchi. Sprinkle with basil leaves, chopped chives, salt, and pepper. If using grated Parmesan, serve separately.

Semolina-based gnocchi are made from a stiff dough that can be cut out with a cookie cutter. They can be baked until crusty, with two kinds of cheese clinging in delicious golden strands. These are really addictive— all you need is a a glass of wine and a cool, green salad for contrast.

# oven-baked
# semolina gnocchi

2 tablespoons extra virgin olive oil

½ cup coarse semolina, plus extra for shaping

1 cup (4 oz.) freshly grated Parmesan cheese

1 cup (4 oz.) freshly grated or finely chopped Gruyère cheese

a handful of fresh flat-leaf parsley, coarsely chopped

¼ teaspoon grated nutmeg

¼–½ teaspoon crumbled hot red pepper flakes (optional)

sea salt

¼ cup extra virgin olive oil, for serving

a plain cookie cutter, 2 inches diameter

a small baking dish, lightly oiled

**Serves 2–3**

Put 1 cup warm water into a large heatproof bowl. Add the olive oil, ½ teaspoon salt, and semolina in that order and, using electric beaters or a balloon whisk, beat well. The oil helps avoid lumps, but work quickly.

Pour the mixture into a large, nonstick skillet and cook over medium heat, stirring constantly with a wooden spoon, until the mixture thickens and forms a paste, about 3 minutes. It will come away from the sides of the pan.

Stir in half the Parmesan and half the Gruyère, parsley, nutmeg, and hot red pepper flakes, if using. Transfer the paste to a work surface dusted with semolina and, using your hands, pat and smooth out the paste to a shape about 8 inches square. Using the cookie cutter, cut out 16 rounds. Lift them out carefully with a spatula.

Arrange in the prepared baking dish in overlapping concentric circles or rows. Sprinkle with the remaining Parmesan and Gruyère and half the olive oil. Bake in a preheated oven at 400°F for 30–35 minutes until hot, crusty, and aromatic. Serve immediately, sprinkled with the remaining olive oil.

Italians adore their pasta, but they also love risotto. Quick to prepare, nutritious, inexpensive, and utterly delicious, risotto is also very versatile—perfect for relaxed, weekday meals or elegant dinner parties.

# basic
# risotto

2 tablespoons extra virgin olive oil

2 tablespoons salted butter

1 onion, sliced

1½ cups risotto rice such as vialone nano, carnaroli, or arborio

½ teaspoon sea salt

4 cups boiling chicken or vegetable stock

flavorings of your choice

**Serves 4**

**1** Heat the oil and butter in a wide saucepan. Add the onion and sauté for 2 minutes until softened and translucent.

**2** Add the rice and stir with a wooden spoon until the grains are well coated and glistening with oil, about 1–2 minutes.

**3** Add the salt and one-third of the boiling stock and bring to a boil. Simmer, stirring, until all the liquid has been absorbed. Continue to add the stock at intervals and cook at a steady simmer, stirring, until all the liquid has been absorbed and the rice is tender, but firm or *al dente* in the center. If you run out of stock, use boiling water to complete cooking the rice.

**4** Mix in flavorings of your choice, such as quartered artichoke hearts, sautéed mushrooms and chicken livers, chopped chives, chopped flat-leaf parsley, and freshly grated Parmesan.

Pumpkin aficionados prefer varieties with green or gray skins: they are drier and denser than the more common orange-skinned pumpkins and butternut squash, giving a more intense flavor and better texture.

# pumpkin risotto

1¼ lb. pumpkin, peeled, seeded, and cut into large chunks, 1 lb. after preparation

2 potatoes, cut into large chunks (optional)

2 tablespoons unsalted butter

milk, as needed

1 quart chicken stock

¼ cup olive oil

2 onions, finely chopped

2 large garlic cloves, crushed

2 cups risotto rice, such as vialone nano, carnaroli, or arborio

sea salt and freshly ground black pepper

**To serve (optional)**

shavings of fresh Parmesan cheese

pumpkin chips*

**Serves 4–6**

Put the pumpkin and potatoes, if using, into a large saucepan and cover with water. Bring to a boil, then simmer until tender. Drain thoroughly and mash with half the butter until creamy—it should have the consistency of thick soup (add milk if necessary).

Put the stock into a large saucepan and heat until almost boiling, then reduce the heat until barely simmering to keep it hot.

Heat the olive oil and remaining butter in a heavy sauté pan, add the onions, and sauté gently until softened and translucent. Add the garlic and cook until lightly golden, about 1–2 minutes. Add the rice and stir with a wooden spoon, until the grains are well coated with oil, about 1–2 minutes. Add one-quarter of the boiling stock and simmer gently, stirring, until all the liquid has been absorbed. Continue to add the stock at intervals and cook at a steady simmer, stirring, until the liquid has been absorbed and the rice is tender, but firm or *al dente* in the center. Stir the cooked pumpkin through the risotto, season to taste, and serve, topped with shavings of Parmesan and pumpkin chips.

**\*Pumpkin chips**  To make pumpkin chips, finely slice segments of pumpkin on a mandoline or with a vegetable peeler (include the skin). Fill a wok or deep-fat fryer one-third full of oil, or to the manufacturer's recommended level. Add the slices of pumpkin, in batches if necessary, and fry until crisp. Remove with a slotted spoon and drain thoroughly on paper towels.

This fragrant, golden risotto is an Italian classic, to serve on its own or as an accompaniment to Osso Buco (page 110). The original *risotto alla milanese* includes beef marrow, which makes it extra-rich.

# saffron risotto

1 quart chicken stock

6 tablespoons salted butter

1 onion, sliced

3–4 garlic cloves, crushed (optional)

2 cups risotto rice, such as vialone nano, carnaroli, or arborio

½ cup white wine

a large pinch of saffron threads

¼ teaspoon sea salt (or, if stock is salty, sugar)

3 oz. fresh Parmesan cheese, shaved with a vegetable peeler

freshly ground black pepper

sprigs of flat-leaf parsley, to serve

**Serves 4**

Put the stock into a large saucepan and heat until almost boiling, then reduce the heat until barely simmering to keep it hot.

Heat 4 tablespoons of the butter in a heavy saucepan, add the onion and garlic, if using, and sauté gently for 1 minute. Add the rice and stir with a wooden spoon until the grains are well coated and glistening with oil, 1–2 minutes. Add the wine and stir until completely absorbed.

Put the saffron and salt or sugar into a small bowl and, using a wooden spoon, grind together, then add 1 ladle of the hot stock. Pour half this mixture into the rice and reserve the remainder. Continue to add the stock at intervals and cook at a steady simmer, stirring, until all the liquid has been absorbed and the rice is tender, but firm or *al dente* in the center, 25–30 minutes. Alternatively, add all the stock at once and cook over a low heat for about 30 minutes, stirring gently from time to time.

Add the remaining 2 tablespoons of butter and the remaining saffron mixture, then stir in half the Parmesan and some black pepper. To serve, sprinkle with the remaining cheese and top with sprigs of parsley.

### Variation

**Wild mushroom risotto** Put 1 oz. broken dried porcini mushrooms and ½ oz. broken dried morel mushrooms into a saucepan and add 1 quart boiling chicken stock. Simmer, covered, for 10–15 minutes until dark and flavorful. Strain the liquid through a cheesecloth and set aside. Rinse the mushroom pieces under cold running water. Proceed as in the main recipe, but use red wine instead of white, and omit the saffron and salt or sugar. The mushrooms should be cooked with the rice.

This risotto is light, fresh, and vibrantly green—a reminder of early summer, when asparagus and peas grow in abundance. Try to use vegetables when they are in season, so that you can enjoy them at their finest and sweetest.

# risotto
## with asparagus, peas, and basil

1 quart vegetable stock

4 tablespoons unsalted butter

1 tablespoon olive oil

8 shallots, finely chopped

1½ cups risotto rice, such as vialone nano, carnaroli, or arborio

¼ cup white wine

12 oz. asparagus, cut into 2-inch lengths

1¼ cups shelled peas, about 6 oz., fresh or frozen

finely grated zest of 1 unwaxed lemon

4 oz. freshly grated Parmesan cheese, plus extra to serve

a large handful of fresh basil, leaves torn, plus extra to serve

sea salt and freshly ground black pepper

**Serves 4**

To prepare the artichokes, pull off the tough outer leaves and, using a sharp knife, cut off the spiky, pointed top. Remove the stalk and cut each artichoke lengthwise into 4 segments if small or 8 if large. Cut away the fuzzy, prickly choke. Squeeze the lemon over the segments to prevent discoloration. Set the artichoke segments aside.

Put the stock into a saucepan and heat until almost boiling, then reduce the heat until barely simmering to keep it hot.

Heat the butter and oil in a heavy sauté pan or casserole. Add the shallots and cook for 1–2 minutes until softened and translucent. Add the garlic and artichoke segments and cook for 2–3 minutes.

Add the rice and stir with a wooden spoon, until the grains are well coated and glistening with oil, about 1–2 minutes. Pour in the wine and stir until completely absorbed.

Add 1 ladle of hot stock and simmer, stirring, until it has been absorbed. Continue to add the stock at intervals and cook at a steady simmer, stirring, until the liquid has been absorbed and the rice is tender, but firm or *al dente* in the centre, about 18–20 minutes.

Add the Parmesan, mascarpone, and parsley, then add salt and pepper to taste. Mix well. Remove from the heat, cover, and let rest for 2 minutes.

Spoon into 4 warmed serving bowls and serve immediately with freshly grated Parmesan.

Try to buy young artichokes with long, uncut stems. The shorter the stem, the tougher the artichoke tends to be. Young artichokes are also less fibrous. Firmly closed artichokes are an indication of freshness: if the leaves are open they are old.

# artichoke risotto

4 small or 2 large globe artichokes
1 lemon, halved
1 quart vegetable stock
4 tablespoons unsalted butter
1 tablespoon olive oil
8 shallots, finely chopped
1 garlic clove, crushed
1½ cups risotto rice, such as vialone nano, carnaroli, or arborio
¼ cup white wine
1 cup (4 oz.) freshly grated Parmesan cheese, plus extra to serve
2 tablespoons mascarpone cheese
a handful of fresh flat-leaf parsley, coarsely chopped
sea salt and freshly ground black pepper

**Serves 4**

To prepare the artichokes, pull off the tough outer leaves and, using a sharp knife, cut off the spiky, pointed top. Remove the stalk and cut each artichoke lengthwise into 4 segments if small or 8 segments if large. Cut away the fuzzy, prickly choke. Squeeze the lemon over the segments to prevent discoloration. Set the artichoke segments aside.

Put the stock into a saucepan and heat until almost boiling, then reduce the heat until barely simmering and keep it hot.

Heat the butter and oil in a heavy sauté pan or casserole over medium heat. Add the shallots and cook for 1–2 minutes until softened but not browned. Add the garlic and artichoke segments and cook for 2–3 minutes.

Add the rice and stir with a wooden spoon, until the grains are well coated and glistening with oil, about 1–2 minutes. Pour in the wine and stir until completely absorbed.

Add a ladle of hot stock and simmer, stirring, until it has been absorbed. Continue to add the stock at intervals and cook as before until the liquid has been absorbed and the rice is tender, but firm or *al dente* in the center, about 18–20 minutes in total.

Add the Parmesan, mascarpone, and parsley, then add salt and pepper to taste. Mix well. Remove from the heat, cover, and let rest for 2 minutes. Spoon into 4 warmed serving bowls and serve immediately with freshly grated Parmesan.

This is a dual-purpose risotto recipe: it produces a traditional saffron risotto and is served hot. If you let it cool, it can be used to make this crisp risotto cake. Saffron threads are best, but Italian gourmet stores sell very good quality saffron powder in little packages—just add it to the boiling stock and proceed as usual (the threads must be steeped in boiling water first).

# italian risotto cake

**Saffron risotto**

4 tablespoons salted butter

1/3 cup extra virgin olive oil

2 leeks, white only, finely sliced

4 garlic cloves, chopped

2 cups risotto rice, such as vialone nano, carnaroli, or arborio

a large pinch of saffron threads, soaked in 1/4 cup boiling water for 10 minutes

1 quart chicken or veal stock

2 oz. freshly grated Parmesan cheese

sea salt

**Risotto cake**

1 lb. cooked, cooled saffron risotto

1 egg yolk, beaten

1 egg, beaten

3 oz. fresh mozzarella cheese, chopped

2–3 tablespoons extra virgin olive oil

**To serve**

freshly cracked black pepper

shavings of fresh Parmesan cheese

arugula, watercress, or radicchio

**Serves 4**

Put the stock into a large saucepan, heat until almost boiling, then reduce the heat until barely simmering to keep it hot.

To make the risotto, heat the butter and olive oil in a large saucepan. Add the leek and garlic and cook gently until softened and translucent. Add the rice and cook, stirring, for about 1–2 minutes until the grains are well coated and glistening with oil. Add all the saffron and its soaking water, then the stock, 1 ladle at a time, and simmer until the liquid has been absorbed before adding another ladle. Stir in the Parmesan and salt and serve immediately, or let cool and use to make the risotto cake.

To make the risotto cake, put the cold risotto, egg yolk, egg, and mozzarella into a bowl and mix carefully—it must be thoroughly amalgamated, but the rice grains should not be broken.

Heat the oil until very hot in a large nonstick skillet, tilting the pan so the oil covers the sides as well as the base. Spoon in the rice mixture, smooth the top, and cook over medium heat for 6–8 minutes or until the base is golden and there is a strong aroma. (Take care that it doesn't burn.) Put a flat saucepan lid or large plate on top and invert the skillet and plate in one quick movement. Slide the rice back in, crust up, and cook the second side until golden.

To serve, cut the cake into wedges. Serve hot or warm, sprinkled with cracked pepper, shavings of Parmesan, and crisp leaves such as arugula, watercress, or radicchio.

secondi piatti

A great dish with assertive flavors and a combination of firm white fish, shellfish, and shrimp. Serve with crusty Italian bread and some light red wine or a peppery white wine, similar to those from the Vesuvius area around the Bay of Naples.

# neapolitan
# seafood stew

4 large garlic cloves, crushed

a bunch of fresh thyme
or rosemary

12 clams

12 mussels

about ¼ cup olive oil

2 medium onions, cut into
wedges through the root

8 ripe, very red tomatoes,
peeled, halved,
and seeded

2 lb. thick boneless white fish
fillets, such as cod

4–8 small whole fish, cleaned
and scaled (optional)

8 uncooked shrimp

1 quart fish stock

sea salt and freshly ground
black pepper

crusty Italian bread, to serve

**Serves 4**

Put 1 cup water into a large, heavy saucepan and add 1 crushed garlic clove and half the herbs. Bring to a boil, then simmer for 2–3 minutes to extract the flavors. Add the clams, cover with a lid, and cook over high heat, shaking the pan from time to time. Remove them as they open so they don't overcook and put onto a plate. Discard any that don't open.

Add the mussels to the pan, cover with a lid, and cook until they open. Remove as they do so and add to the plate with the clams. Discard any that don't open. Strain the cooking stock through cheesecloth into a bowl to remove the grit. Set aside.

Heat the olive oil in a large skillet, add the onion wedges, and cook until lightly browned on both sides. Reduce the heat and cook until softened. Stir in the remaining garlic and cook for a few minutes until golden. Add lots of black pepper, then add the tomatoes, the remaining herbs, both kinds of fish, and the shrimp. Pour in the stock and bring to boiling point. Reduce the heat and simmer for a few minutes until the fish turns opaque. Add the mussels, clams, and the strained mussel poaching liquid and reheat, then add salt and pepper to taste.

Ladle into 4 large, warmed bowls and serve with crusty Italian bread.

A taste of the Mediterranean—whole fish or fillets wrapped in foil and cooked on an outdoor grill until tender. Serve them with olive oil flavored with garlic, capers, lemon juice, and anchovy—an intense effect that's not for the faint-hearted!

# sea bass packages

4 medium sea bass or snapper, about 10 oz. each, or 4 fillets, 6 oz. each

freshly squeezed juice of 1 lemon, plus extra to taste

½ cup extra virgin olive oil

8 canned anchovy fillets, chopped

2 garlic cloves, chopped

¼ cup small capers in brine, drained

a small handful of fresh flat-leaf parsley, chopped

sea salt and freshly ground black pepper

*4 sheets of foil, 10 inches wide, brushed with oil*

*a large baking tray*

**Serves 4**

Using a sharp knife, make 2 diagonal slashes in both sides of each fish and rub in salt and black pepper. Set each fish onto a sheet of oiled foil and sprinkle with half the lemon juice. Take the long edges of foil and pinch and roll together into form a tight seal. Loosely pleat or fold the foil lengthwise, then crunch and roll the narrow ends until tightly closed. Put the packages onto a large baking tray.

Bake the packages in a preheated oven at 350°F for 10–15 minutes for fillets or about 20–25 minutes for whole fish, or until the flesh is white and firm (open one package to test). Alternatively, cook on a preheated outdoor grill over medium-hot coals for 8–12 minutes for whole fish or 6–8 minutes for fillets.

Meanwhile, put the remaining lemon juice, olive oil, anchovies, and garlic into a blender and process to form a purée. Alternatively, use a pestle and mortar. Pour the mixture into a mixing bowl, then stir in the capers and parsley. Add extra lemon juice to taste.

Put the fish packages onto 4 large, warmed serving plates. Open each one just enough to spoon in the sauce, then reseal and serve.

For the best flavor and texture, choose a free-range bird for this dish. You can roast it first on one side, then the other, then breast up for the final stage. Don't worry about the amount of garlic—when it's roasted like this, it becomes sweet and nutty.

# italian roast chicken

2½–3 lb. chicken

2 tablespoons unsalted butter

4 garlic cloves, well crushed, plus 4 whole heads of garlic (optional)

melted butter or olive oil, for brushing

½ cup robust red wine

sea salt and freshly ground black pepper

**Serves 4**

Using your fingers, work the skin of the chicken loose over the breast and thighs. Wiggle the wishbone free and cut it out, trying not to puncture the skin. This will make it easier to carve.

Put the butter and crushed garlic into a small mixing bowl and blend well. Push some of the mixture under the breast skin and leg skin. Skewer the neck skin closed underneath. Season the bird all over with salt and black pepper. Slice the tops off the whole heads of garlic, if using, cutting them partly through, and brush them all over with melted butter or olive oil. Set aside.

Set the bird in a large roasting pan, or on a roasting rack in the pan. Roast in a preheated oven at 425°F for 45 minutes, then add the whole garlic heads and reduce the oven temperature to 375°F. Roast for a further 30 minutes. To test the chicken, pierce the thigh in the thickest part with a skewer. The juices should run clear and golden. If the juices still look at all pink, cook a little longer.

Transfer the chicken to a large serving dish, add the whole roasted garlic, if using, and put the dish into the oven. Turn off the heat and leave the door slightly open. Set the roasting pan on top of the stove over a high heat and stir in the wine, scraping up all the sediment from the base of the pan. Boil down until syrupy. Serve this simple sauce with the roast chicken. The sweet, soft, roasted garlic cloves should be squeezed out of their papery coatings and eaten with the chicken.

Polpette—meatballs—are made all over Italy using finely ground lamb, beef, veal, or pork with whatever accents suit them best: cheese, herbs, sausage, capers, citrus zest, pine nuts, chile, and even anchovy. In Sicily, lemon leaves are common, but you can substitute grated or finely sliced lemon zest. Before cooking, either roll the meatballs in grated zest, or insert sliced zest.

# polpette al limone

1 lb. lean lamb, ground twice

8 oz. luganega or other coarse Italian sausage, removed from its casing

2 slices of stale Italian bread, about 3 oz.

beef stock or water, for dipping the bread

1 egg, beaten

a small handful of flat-leaf parsley, chopped

4 garlic cloves, chopped

½ teaspoon ground allspice, mace, or nutmeg

1 teaspoon sea salt

⅓ cup freshly grated Parmesan cheese

freshly ground black pepper

24 fresh lemon leaves (optional)

juice and zest of 1 lemon (see method)

about ½ cup olive oil, for frying

stock, wine, or water, to deglaze the pan

creamy mashed potato, to serve

*24 toothpicks*

**Serves 4**

Put the lamb and sausage meat into a large bowl and, using a wooden spoon, mix thoroughly. Put the bread into another bowl, pour over the stock or water, and let soak for 2 minutes. Squeeze dry and crumble in with the meats. Add the beaten egg, parsley, garlic, spice, salt, cheese, and black pepper. Beat and knead to a smooth paste, then using wet (or oiled) hands, divide into 24 balls. Pinch and squeeze to make them compact, then flatten slightly. If using lemon leaves, fasten one onto each ball with a toothpick. Alternatively, roll the balls in grated lemon zest or insert a strip of zest.

Heat half the olive oil in a large, nonstick skillet. Add half the polpette and sauté for about 2–3 minutes on each side until golden, firm, and aromatic. Remove from the pan, keep hot, and repeat with the remaining olive oil and polpette. Squeeze the juice of the lemon into the skillet and add a little stock, wine, or water to dissolve the pan sediment. Pour the pan juices over the polpette and serve with creamy mashed potato.

Well-cooked osso buco, braised shank of veal, is so tender it can be eaten with a spoon. *Oss bus* in Milanese dialect means "bone with a hole"—inside the hole is the creamy bone marrow that's the choicest part of the dish. Get your butcher to cut slices of veal shank, about 2 inches thick, then tie up the pieces with twine so the marrow doesn't fall out during cooking. This authentic version doesn't contain tomatoes—it is flavored instead with anchovy and sprinkled with gremolata, made from lemon zest, parsley, and garlic.

# osso buco

8 pieces of veal shank, 2 inches thick (tied up with kitchen twine to keep in the marrow)

⅓ cup all purpose flour, seasoned with salt and pepper

⅓ cup extra virgin olive oil

4 tablespoons unsalted butter

2 onions, sliced into rings

2 carrots, chopped or sliced

2 celery stalks, chopped or sliced

6 salted or 8 canned anchovies, rinse and chopped

1–2 cups white wine

1 cup veal, beef, or chicken stock

a small bunch of fresh herbs, such as parsley, thyme, bay leaf, and lovage tied together

sea salt and freshly ground black pepper

**Gremolata topping**

finely grated zest of ½ lemon

a small bunch of fresh flat-leaf parsley, chopped

2 garlic cloves, crushed

**Serves 4–6**

Choose a flameproof casserole or lidded skillet into which the meat will fit snugly. Put the meat onto a board and dust with the flour on both sides. Heat the olive oil in the casserole or skillet. Add the meat and brown for 5 minutes on each side, turning carefully.

Heat the butter in another skillet. Add the onions, carrots, and celery and brown for a few minutes. Add the anchovies and mash with a wooden spoon. Add the wine and let bubble for 2 minutes.

Remove the meat from the casserole with a slotted spoon. Add half the vegetable-anchovy mixture to the casserole, put the veal on top, then pour the remaining vegetable-anchovy mixture over the top. Trickle the stock down the sides of the pan until the meat is nearly covered, then add the bunch of herbs. Bring to a boil, cover, reduce the heat to very low, and simmer for 1½–2 hours on top of the stove. Alternatively, bake in a preheated oven at 300°F for 2½ hours.

To make the gremolata, put the lemon zest, parsley, and garlic into a bowl and mix well. When the meat is tender, cut the twine and serve the pieces in large, warmed soup plates. Spoon some of the sauce over each helping, then add the gremolata topping.

**Variation**

This recipe can also be made with lamb shanks. Allow 1–2 shanks per person, depending on size.

This elegant dish combines rich and fascinating flavors—beef, truffle oil, thyme, garlic, and full-flavored portobello mushrooms. The sliced rare beef is set on a pleasantly peppery salad. Really good estate-bottled extra virgin is crucial—together with earthy, distinctive truffle oil, it transforms this dish into a gourmet event.

# char-grilled beef fillet
## with portobello mushrooms

4 filet mignon, 8 oz. each, well aged, at room temperature

6 tablespoons extra virgin olive oil

2 tablespoons truffle oil

1 tablespoon sherry vinegar

1 teaspoon black peppercorns, coarsely crushed

a small bunch of fresh thyme sprigs

4 large portobello mushrooms

2 garlic cloves, crushed

sea salt flakes, crushed

**Salad**

2 handfuls of arugula

2 handfuls of watercress

2 handfuls of lamb's lettuce

4 oz. red radishes, sliced crosswise

4 oz. fresh Parmesan cheese, cut into long shavings with a vegetable peeler

*a stove-top grill pan*

**Serves 4**

Pat the beef dry with paper towels. Put it into a plastic bag, add 3 tablespoons of the olive oil, the truffle oil, vinegar, crushed peppercorns, and thyme. Using your fingers, knead gently together. Seal the bag loosely and set aside to marinate in the refrigerator for 30 minutes.

To make the salad, put the arugula, watercress, lamb's lettuce, radishes, and Parmesan into a bowl and toss gently. Pile onto 4 serving plates and drizzle with the remaining 3 tablespoons olive oil.

Remove the beef from the bag, drain, then put into a preheated stove-top grill pan or large, nonstick skillet. Alternatively, cook on a preheated outdoor grill over medium-hot coals. Put the mushrooms into the plastic bag, add the garlic and 1 teaspoon of crushed sea salt flakes, and, using your fingers, turn until the marinade is evenly absorbed.

Cook the beef fillets for 5–6 minutes on each side or until well marked in lines, aromatic, and dark, but still pink inside. Transfer to a large plate and let stand, covered, while you cook the mushrooms.

Add the mushrooms to the pan or grill and cook for 2–3 minutes on each side or until dark and aromatic. (If any marinade is left in the bag, pour it into the cupped side of the mushrooms first.)

To serve, slice each fillet crosswise into 5–6 slices. Arrange the sliced fillets on top of the salad. Add the mushrooms, halved or quartered, then serve.

# contorni

There are as many variations of this Tuscan bread salad as there are cooks. The secret is to let the flavors blend well without the bread disintegrating into a mush. Always use the ripest, reddest, most flavorful tomatoes you can find, such as Italian plum tomatoes or the juicy heirloom varieties found at summertime farmers' markets.

# tuscan panzanella

6 very ripe plum tomatoes

2 garlic cloves, finely sliced

¾ cup extra virgin olive oil

4 thick slices of day-old bread, preferably Italian-style such as puglièse or ciabatta

4 inches cucumber, halved, seeded, and finely sliced diagonally

1 red onion, chopped

1 tablespoon chopped fresh flat-leaf parsley

2 tablespoons white wine vinegar, cider vinegar, or sherry vinegar

1 teaspoon balsamic vinegar (optional)

a bunch of fresh basil, leaves torn

12 caperberries or 4 tablespoons capers packed in brine, rinsed and drained

sea salt and freshly ground black pepper

*a baking tray, lightly oiled*

*a stove-top grill pan*

**Serves 4**

Cut the tomatoes in half, spike with slivers of garlic, and arrange on the baking tray. Sprinkle with a little of the olive oil and roast in a preheated oven at 350°F for about 1 hour, or until wilted and some of the moisture has evaporated.

Meanwhile, put the bread onto a preheated stove-top grill pan and cook until lightly toasted and charred with marks on both sides. Tear or cut the toast into pieces and put into a large salad bowl. Sprinkle with a little water until damp.

Add the tomatoes, cucumber, onion, and parsley, then add salt and black pepper to taste. Sprinkle with the the remaining olive oil and vinegar, toss well, then set aside for about 1 hour to develop the flavors.

Add the fresh basil leaves and caperberries or capers and serve.

In Italian markets, you see boxes of different baby leaves. Shoppers choose a handful each of their favorite kinds to make a mixed salad. Originally, the mixture was picked from wild plants in the fields (*campo* means "field") and still is in country areas, so the mixture should include herbs, bitter leaves, soft greens, and crunchy leaves. In my supermarket, I find it best to choose mesclun, then add extra watercress and arugula.

# insalata di campo

about 12 oz. wild leaves and herbs or mesclun

1 tablespoon balsamic vinegar

6–8 tablespoons extra virgin olive oil

freshly squeezed juice of ½ lemon

sea salt and freshly ground black pepper

2 oz. Parmesan cheese, in the piece, to serve

**Serves 4–6**

Wash the leaves well in a large bowl of cold water. Drain and shake or spin dry without crushing or bruising them. Transfer to a clean cloth lined with paper towels, wrap in the cloth, and keep in the refrigerator for about 30 minutes.

Put the vinegar, oil, and lemon juice into a small bowl, then add salt and black pepper to taste, and beat well.

Using a swivel-bladed vegetable peeler, remove long, thin curls of Parmesan from the block, then set them aside.

When ready to serve, put the leaves into a large salad bowl. Beat the dressing briefly and sprinkle over the salad. Toss gently until everything gleams, then top with the shavings of Parmesan and serve.

**Note** Choose a combination of leaves—whatever is fresh and good on the day. Suggestions include arugula, young dandelion leaves, lamb's lettuce, flat-leaf parsley, baby spinach, sprigs of fresh dill, and, if you have a garden, nasturtium leaves.

We have found that the bell peppers stuffed with melted goat cheese are a particular favorite with guests, especially vegetarians—serve three halves with a few arugula leaves as an easy, spectacular appetizer, even for a formal dinner party, or this way as an accompaniment to entrées.

# stuffed roasted peppers
## with goat cheese, pesto, and roasted vegetables

1 lb. butternut squash or green-skinned pumpkin, cut into 1-inch wedges

2 sweet potatoes, cut into 1-inch chunks

2 red onions, quartered lengthwise into wedges

½ cup extra virgin olive oil, plus extra for sprinkling

4 medium tomatoes, halved

sea salt flakes and freshly ground black pepper

**Stuffed bell peppers**

2 red and 2 yellow bell peppers, halved and seeded

a handful of fresh basil leaves

8 cherry tomatoes, halved

8 teaspoons Classic Basil Pesto (page 71)

about 4 oz. aged goat cheese, cut into 8 chunks

**To serve**

lemon wedges

ciabatta or focaccia bread, char-grilled

**Serves 4–8**

To make the stuffed bell peppers, brush a large roasting pan with olive oil and add the peppers, cut side up. Put a basil leaf, a halved cherry tomato, a spoonful of pesto, and a chunk of goat cheese into each pepper half.

Put the butternut squash or pumpkin, sweet potatoes, and red onions into a plastic bag, add the ½ cup olive oil, salt, and pepper, then shake until everything is well coated in oil. Add them to the roasting pan, leaving space around each piece (use 2 roasting pans if necessary), then add the tomato halves. Sprinkle with salt, pepper, and olive oil.

Put the pan or pans into a preheated oven at 400°F or as high as your oven will go, and roast for about 30 minutes or until all the vegetables are tender and brown at the edges.

Serve with fresh basil leaves, lemon wedges, and char-grilled ciabatta.

You can part-prepare the chickpeas, so the dressing soaks in well, then add the fresh ingredients just before serving. You can add any number of other ingredients, including olives, prosciutto, salami or chorizo, canned tuna, other vegetables, leaves, or herbs, and a few of your favorite spices. Whatever looks good that day.

# chickpea salad

4 cups (2 cans, 15 oz. each) cooked or canned chickpeas, rinsed and drained

¾ cup (6½ oz. jar) marinated artichoke hearts

8 oz. sun-blushed (semi-dried) tomatoes (optional)*

8 oz. very ripe cherry tomatoes, halved

8 scallions, finely sliced diagonally

fresh basil leaves, torn

a small bunch of fresh chives, snipped

fresh flat-leaf parsley, chopped

2 oz. Parmesan cheese, shaved

1 tablespoon black pepper, cracked with a mortar and pestle

**Dressing**

⅓ cup extra virgin olive oil

1 tablespoon freshly squeezed lemon juice

1 teaspoon Dijon mustard (optional)

1 small garlic clove, crushed

sea salt and freshly ground black pepper

**Serves 4**

Put all the dressing ingredients into a mixing bowl and beat with a fork or small whisk. Alternatively, put into a screw-top bottle and shake well to form an emulsion.

Put the chickpeas, artichoke hearts, and sun-blushed tomatoes, if using, into a bowl. Pour over the dressing and stir. Cover with a lid or plastic wrap and chill for up to 4 hours.

When ready to serve, add the cherry tomatoes, scallions, basil, chives, and parsley. Stir gently, then sprinkle with shavings of Parmesan and black pepper.

**\*Note** Sun-blushed tomatoes, which are partly dried sun-dried tomatoes, are sold in Italian gourmet stores.

# italian dressings

## vinaigrette

1 tablespoon white or red
wine vinegar

5 tablespoons extra virgin
olive oil

sea salt and freshly ground
white pepper

**Serves 4**

Put all the ingredients into a mixing bowl or screw-top bottle and beat or shake well, using a fork or wire whisk to form an emulsion.

To make a smaller amount—enough for a salad—use 1 part vinegar to 5 parts oil, plus seasoning to taste. If preferred, pour the ingredients into the salad bowl and beat them with a fork. Put the salad on top and leave undisturbed (no longer than 30 minutes), then toss just before serving.

## extra virgin olive oil

Dispense with any acidity at all: simply pour superb, estate-bottled olive oil over the hot or warm food—roasts, barbecued fish, warm vegetables, pasta, risotto and couscous. Even better, serve in small bowls with lots of fresh crusty bread for dipping—heaven!

## mayonnaise

2 egg yolks, at room
temperature

2 teaspoons Dijon mustard

¼ teaspoon sea salt

2 teaspoons fresh lemon
juice or
white wine vinegar

¾ cup extra virgin olive oil

½ cup safflower oil or other
light oil

**Serves 4**

Put the yolks into a medium bowl. Stir in the mustard, salt, and half the lemon juice or vinegar and beat until smooth. Mix the oils in a measuring cup, then gradually pour the oil into the bowl, beating constantly to form a stiff, glossy emulsion. When all the oil has been added, taste, then beat in the remaining lemon juice or vinegar if necessary. Taste and adjust the seasoning.

Alternatively, to make in a blender or food processor, add 1 extra whole egg to the main recipe—the position of the blades means there is inadequate friction, so you need extra volume. This method works very well, though the emulsion is denser and less fluffy.

dolci

A superb basic Italian gelato recipe, made with cream rather than milk. It produces rather a large quantity, so divide the mixture into two or three parts, add a different flavoring to each, then churn separately.

# gelato di crema

1 quart heavy cream
or light cream

5 egg yolks

1¼ cups sugar

**Choice of flavourings**

¼ cup liqueur, such as
Italian Strega,
Grand Marnier,
sweet Marsala wine,
dark or golden rum,

fruit juices or purées, such
as pineapple, passionfruit
pulp, peach, mandarin,
blackberry, raspberry

*an ice cream machine or
shallow freezer-proof boxes*

**Makes about 1½ quarts**

Pour the cream into a small, heavy saucepan and heat gently.

Put the egg yolks and sugar into a large mixing bowl and, using electric beaters or balloon whisk, beat until pale and creamy. Beat 2 tablespoons of the hot cream into the egg mixture to warm the yolks, then beat in the remaining cream, little by little.

Pour into the top of a double boiler, or into a heatproof bowl set over a saucepan of simmering water. Cook over gentle heat, stirring constantly, until the mixture is thick enough to coat the back of a spoon. Do not let boil, or the mixture will curdle.

Let cool, then chill in the refrigerator until very cold. Transfer to an ice cream machine and churn.* Serve immediately or transfer to a freezer-proof container and freeze for later use.

If you don't have an ice cream machine, pour the mixture into shallow freezer-proof boxes and let partly freeze until ice crystals form around the edges. Remove from the freezer and beat with a fork or blender. Return to the freezer and partly freeze again. The more you freeze and beat, the smoother the ice cream will be.

Let soften in the refrigerator for about 20 minutes before serving.

**\*Note** If you wish to add flavorings, add them just before churning.

Italian gelati are often made with milk, and so are denser than when made with cream. When made with a mixture of cream and milk, as here, they are even more delicious. Both this recipe and the one on the previous page are very good with just vanilla, but you can add other flavors, such as finely chopped chocolate.

# traditional gelato

2 cups milk

2 vanilla beans or ¼ teaspoon vanilla extract (optional)

3 egg yolks

⅔ cup sugar

1 cup heavy cream

*an ice cream machine or shallow freezer-proof boxes*

**Makes about 1 quart**

Put the milk and vanilla, if using, into a heavy saucepan and heat to just below boiling point. Remove from the heat and set aside to infuse for 15 minutes. Remove the vanilla beans, if using.

Put the egg yolks into a mixing bowl and, using electric beaters or balloon whisk, beat until creamy. Beat 2 tablespoons of the hot milk into the egg mixture, to warm the yolks, then beat in the remaining milk, a little at a time. Stir in the sugar, then transfer to the top of a double boiler or a heatproof bowl set over a saucepan of simmering water. Cook over gentle heat, stirring constantly, until the mixture is thick enough to coat the back of a wooden spoon. Do not let boil, or the mixture will curdle.

Remove from the heat and dip the pan into a bowl of cold water to stop the cooking process. Let cool completely, stir in the cream, then transfer to an ice cream machine and churn.* Serve immediately or transfer to a freezer-proof container and freeze.

If you don't have an ice cream machine, pour the mixture into shallow freezer-proof boxes and let partly freeze until ice crystals form around the edges. Remove from the freezer and beat with a fork or blender. Return to the freezer and partly freeze again. The more you freeze and beat, the smoother the ice cream will be.

Let soften in the refrigerator for 20 minutes before serving.

**\*Note** If adding flavorings, add them just before churning.

Tiramisu is probably Italy's most famous dessert, and beloved of those with a sweet tooth, wherever they live. It is the basis of this thoroughly wicked concoction. Sweet Marsala wine is the traditional flavoring, but rum could also be used.

# gelato di tiramisu

8 ladyfingers

sweet Marsala wine or rum (see method)

3–6 tablespoons strong espresso coffee, chilled

1 cup mascarpone cheese

**Zabaglione gelato**

⅔ cup sugar

3 egg yolks

1 cup heavy cream

¼ cup sweet Marsala wine

**To decorate**

whipped cream

shaved dark chocolate

*an ice cream machine*
*2 freezer-proof boxes*

**Serves 4**

To make the zabaglione gelato, put the sugar and 1 cup water into a small, heavy saucepan and cook over medium heat until the sugar has completely dissolved. Remove from the heat. Put the egg yolks into a bowl and, using a electric beaters or balloon whisk, beat until pale and creamy. Beat 2 tablespoons of the hot syrup into the eggs to warm the yolks, then gradually beat the egg mixture back into the syrup—the mixture will froth, like zabaglione. Using a spoon, fold in the cream and Marsala, then transfer to an ice cream machine and churn*. Transfer to a plastic freezer-proof box. Freeze.

Put the Marsala or rum into a small bowl, then dip in the sponge fingers. Break or chop into pieces and put into the second box.

Put the mascarpone and 3 tablespoons of the coffee into a bowl and mix well. Taste, then add more coffee, if preferred. Spoon over the top of the sponge fingers. Chill until ready to serve.

To serve, remove the gelato from the freezer and dip into warm water so it can be unmolded. Transfer it to the top of the mascarpone mixture, then invert the whole mixture onto a serving plate. Cut into slices and decorate each slice with whipped cream and shaved chocolate.

Just before serving, remove from the refrigerator, dip the box into a bowl of warm water so it's easier to remove, then invert it onto a rectangular serving plate. Decorate with whipped cream and shaved dark chocolate and serve immediately. To cut slices, dip a sharp knife in hot water, wipe dry with a cloth, then cut slices, making sure everyone gets a share of the cream and chocolate.

**\*Note** If you don't have an ice cream machine, see page 129 for the freezing method.

This lemon sorbet is very sweet—so if you prefer yours more tart, reduce the quantity of sugar. Strain the mixture before churning if you like, but many people like the extra zip of the lemon zest. When grating the zest, for this or any other sorbet, make sure none of the white pith is included, or the sorbetto will be unpleasantly bitter. An egg white, beaten to a froth, is often stirred into sorbetti before freezing, to lighten the texture.

# sorbetto al limone

1¼ cups sugar,
or to taste

grated zest of 2 lemons

2 cups freshly
squeezed lemon juice

*an ice cream machine
or freezer-proof boxes*

**Makes about 1 quart**

Put ½ cup water, sugar, and lemon zest into a small, heavy saucepan and cook over medium heat, stirring constantly, until the sugar has dissolved.

Let cool, chill in the refrigerator, then add the lemon juice. Strain, then put into an ice cream machine and churn. Serve immediately or transfer to a freezer-proof container and freeze for later use. Let soften in the refrigerator for 15 minutes before serving.

**Variations**

**Lime sorbetto**  Substitute the same quantity of lime juice and zest for the lemon, then proceed as in the main recipe.

**Mandarin sorbetto**  Substitute 2 cups mandarin or tangerine juice for the freshly squeezed lemon juice. Use the grated zest of 2 mandarins instead of the lemons and proceed as in the main recipe.

**Blood orange sorbetto**  Substitute 2 cups orange juice for the mandarin juice, preferably from red blood oranges, and the grated zest of 1 orange, and proceed as in the main recipe.

This is one of Italy's most famous desserts. Make it just before you want to serve it, and make sure you are organized before you start—provide a green salad for your guests while you work in the kitchen, or there may be a riot while they wait!

# zabaglione

5 egg yolks
1 egg
½ cup sugar
½ cup Marsala wine
8–12 amaretti cookies
or *Brutti ma buoni*
(see below), for serving

**Serves 4–6**

**Brutti ma buoni**

*Ugly-but-good cookies*

1½ lb. almond paste,
coarsely grated
2 egg whites
2 oz. candied orange
peel, finely chopped
4 oz. candied lemon
peel, finely chopped
1 oz. unskinned
almonds, chopped
4 tablespoons
(1 oz.) pine nuts
confectioners' sugar,
for dusting

*a large baking tray*

**Makes 32**

Put the egg yolks, egg, and sugar into a heatproof bowl set over a saucepan of barely simmering water and stir well. Using electric beaters, balloon whisk, or rotary beater, beat the mixture until it becomes first a stable, light froth, then a thick mousse-like consistency, about 10–15 minutes. Add the Marsala, 1 tablespoon at a time, beating constantly. (Check the water level from time to time—it tends to evaporate. Do not overfill when you top it up—the bowl and water must never touch.)

Remove the saucepan and bowl from the heat and continue beating until the froth will hold its shape and stay thick when the beaters are lifted out. Serve warm in tall goblets or pretty tumblers set on small plates, with cookies for dipping.

## Brutti ma buoni

Put the almond paste and egg whites into a mixing bowl and, using a wooden spoon, beat well. Add the candied peels and stir briefly. Chill for 30 minutes.

Dust your hands with confectioners' sugar. Take 1 teaspoon of the dough and roll it in one hand, pushing in some nuts with the other. Arrange 2 inches apart on an ungreased baking tray and bake in a preheated oven at 300°F for 30 minutes until golden and firm. Remove from the oven and let cool on the baking tray, then transfer to wire racks and let cool completely. Store in an airtight container. Serve dusted with confectioners' sugar.

## Variation

To serve as a *Semifreddo de Zabaglione*, beat the warm zabaglione until cool, then fold gently into 1¼ cups cream, firmly whipped. Freeze without stirring. To churn in an ice cream machine, do not whip the cream before folding together. Churn until set, about 20 minutes.

This Mediterranean cake comes from Sicily, where they use olive oil instead of butter to make cakes. It can be served as a dessert—with a scoop of citrus sorbet or gelato—or as a cake with an espresso and a glass of ice-cold water. It is also wonderful with a glass of Italian lemon liqueur—Limoncello from the Naples area, or Limuneddu di Sicilia. Cointreau or Grand Marnier are good alternatives.

# lemon polenta cake

shredded or grated zest and juice of 1 lemon

shredded or grated zest and juice of 1 orange

¾ cup extra virgin olive oil

1 cup plus 1 tablespoon sugar

¼ teaspoon salt

3 large eggs

1½ cups semolina

1 teaspoon baking powder

4 oz. ground almonds or slivered almonds ground to a powder in a small blender

1 teaspoon almond extract

¼ cup Cointreau or Grand Marnier

*a springform cake pan, 9 inches diameter, lightly oiled and bottom lined with parchment paper*

**Serves 8–12**

Reserve a little of the shredded lemon and orange zest and put the remainder into a bowl with the orange and lemon juice, olive oil, sugar, salt, and eggs. Using electric beaters or balloon whisk, beat until light and fluffy and doubled in volume.

Sift the semolina and baking powder into a second bowl and add the ground almonds. Stir the almond extract into the egg mixture. Pour all at once into the dry ingredients and fold together, but do not overmix. Spoon into the prepared cake pan and smooth the surface.

Bake towards the top of a preheated oven at 325°F for 40–45 minutes or until pale gold at the edges and firm in the center. A skewer pushed into the middle of the cake should come out clean.

Remove from the oven and let cool in the pan for about 10 minutes. Sprinkle the liqueur and reserved shredded zest over the top. Push the cake out, still on its loose metal base, and let cool on a wire rack for another 10 minutes. Remove the base and paper. Serve in wedges, warm or cool, but not chilled.

A wonderful pick-me-up on a hot summer afternoon—and one that can be easily adapted to other ingredients, such as tomato juice, orange and raspberry juice, and so on. Even if you don't usually take sugar in your coffee, you will probably prefer it in this granita.

# coffee granita

5–6 tablespoons freshly ground coffee

1 quart boiling water

sugar, to taste

**To serve (optional)**

6 tablespoons whipped cream

2 oz. bittersweet chocolate, shaved

*an 8-cup French press*

*a shallow freezer-proof box*

**Serves 6**

Put the coffee into the French press and pour over the boiling water. Let brew for 3 minutes, then press the plunger and pour into a heatproof bowl or pitcher and stir in sugar to taste—it should be sweeter than you would usually like. Let cool, then transfer to the freezer-proof box and freeze.

When the mixture is frozen but not rock-hard, remove from the freezer. Using a sturdy fork, crush and break the frozen coffee into icy shards. Spoon the frappé into large coffee cups or tall glasses. Serve immediately either plain or topped with whipped cream and shaved dark chocolate.

**Variations**

Put ½ cup chilled espresso coffee, 2 scoops vanilla ice cream, and ½ cup milk into a blender and blend well. Add sugar to taste and pour into 2 tall glasses.

Substitute crushed pineapple, pear or apricot nectar, or orange and raspberry juice for the espresso coffee.

# index

# conversion charts

Weights and measures have been rounded up or down slightly to make measuring easier.

## volume equivalents

| American | Metric | Imperial |
|---|---|---|
| 1 teaspoon | 5 ml | |
| 1 tablespoon | 15 ml | |
| 1/4 cup | 60 ml | 2 fl. oz. |
| 1/3 cup | 75 ml | 2 1/2 fl. oz. |
| 1/2 cup | 125 ml | 4 fl. oz. |
| 2/3 cup | 150 ml | 5 fl. oz. (1/4 pint) |
| 3/4 cup | 175 ml | 6 fl. oz. |
| 1 cup | 250 ml | 8 fl. oz. |

## weight equivalents          measurements

| Imperial | Metric | Inches | Cm |
|---|---|---|---|
| 1 oz. | 25 g | 1/4 inch | 5 mm |
| 2 oz. | 50 g | 1/2 inch | 1 cm |
| 3 oz. | 75 g | 3/4 inch | 1.5 cm |
| 4 oz. | 125 g | 1 inch | 2.5 cm |
| 5 oz. | 150 g | 2 inches | 5 cm |
| 6 oz. | 175 g | 3 inches | 7 cm |
| 7 oz. | 200 g | 4 inches | 10 cm |
| 8 oz. (1/2 lb.) | 250 g | 5 inches | 12 cm |
| 9 oz. | 275 g | 6 inches | 15 cm |
| 10 oz. | 300 g | 7 inches | 18 cm |
| 11 oz. | 325 g | 8 inches | 20 cm |
| 12 oz. | 375 g | 9 inches | 23 cm |
| 13 oz. | 400 g | 10 inches | 25 cm |
| 14 oz. | 425 g | 11 inches | 28 cm |
| 15 oz. | 475 g | 12 inches | 30 cm |
| 16 oz. (1 lb.) | 500 g | | |
| 2 1b. | 1 kg | | |

## oven temperatures

| | | |
|---|---|---|
| 110°C | (225°F) | Gas 1/4 |
| 120°C | (250°F) | Gas 1/2 |
| 140°C | (275°F) | Gas 1 |
| 150°C | (300°F) | Gas 2 |
| 160°C | (325°F) | Gas 3 |
| 180°C | (350°F) | Gas 4 |
| 190°C | (375°F) | Gas 5 |
| 200°C | (400°F) | Gas 6 |
| 220°C | (425°F) | Gas 7 |
| 230°C | (450°F) | Gas 8 |
| 240°C | (475°F) | Gas 9 |

# acknowledgments

**Recipes**

**Silvana Franco**
Tomato focaccia, Basic pizza dough, Roasted pepper pizza, Eggplant with bresaola, arugula, and parmesan, Quattro stagioni, Topsy turvy cherry tomato pizza, Prosciutto, rosemary, and goat cheese pizza, Wafer potato pizza, Pizza marinara, Mushroom with basil, chile, and garlic, Homemade pasta, Classic basil pesto, Classic tomato sauce, White spaghetti, Pasta con le vongole, Pasta e fagioli, Classic lasagne.

**Ursula Ferrigno**
Saffron risotto, Risotto with asparagus, peas, and basil, Artichoke risotto.

**Clare Ferguson**
Bagna cauda, Peperoni farciti, Black olives sott'olio, Green olives with fennel, Mussels with garlic, parsley, and lemon, Clams with chile parsley sauce, Focaccia with olives, Semolina gnocchi, Gnocchi with tomato sauce, Basic risotto, Sea bass packages, Italian roast chicken, Polpetti al limone/meatballs with lemon, Osso buco, Char-grilled beef fillet, Italian risotto cake, The vinaigrette family, Insalata di campo, Zabaglione, Lemon polenta cake.

**Elsa Petersen-Schepelern**
Anchovy pastry pinwheels, Spice-speckled cheese straws, Mini pizzas, Grilled Italian antipasto, Tonno e fagioli, Insalata gonzaga, Italian pumpkin bean soup, Tuscan ribollita, Pumpkin soup, Italian mushroom soup, Fettuccine with pesto and gorgonzola sauce, Pumpkin risotto, Neapolitan seafood stew, Tuscan panzanella, Warm roasted vegetable salad, Chickpea salad, Gelato di crema, Rich traditional gelato, Gelato di tiramisu, Sorbetto al limone, Coffee granita.

**Photography**

**Peter Cassidy**
Pages 2–3, 4–5, 6–7, 17, 18, 21–23, 25, 26, 29, 30, 35, 39 above left, 70, 84, 88 below left, above left and right,100–101, 104, 107, 113–115,117, 118, 121, 122, 124, 138.

**William Lingwood**
Page 1, 8–11, 13, 14, 32–33, 36, 39 above right, below left and below right, 40, 42–43, 44–46, 49–51, 53, 54, 64, 73, 74, 79, 80, 83.

**Jeremy Hopley**
Pages 61, 67, 68 above left, below left and right, 77, 86, 91, 92, 99, 103, 108, 111, 137.

**James Merrell**
Pages 126–128, 131,132, 134, 141, 144.

**Debi Treloar**
Pages 58, 63 and endpapers.

**Jason Lowe**
Pages 56–57, 88 below right, 95, 96.

Recipes in this book were previously published in other Ryland Peters & Small cookbooks, including *Pizza* and *Pasta* by Silvana Franco; *Risotto* by Ursula Ferrigno; *Chicken: from Maryland to Kiev, Antipasti, Extra Virgin: Cooking with Olive Oil,* and *Flavors of Italy* by Clare Ferguson; *Fingerfood, Grill Pan Cooking, Salads, Pumpkin Butternut and Squash, Meal in a Bowl, Soups, Gelato Sorbet and Ice Cream,* and *Smoothies and Other Blended Drinks* by Elsa Petersen-Schepelern.